D1368504

The
Irish-American
Heritage

David M. Brownstone

Part of the America's Ethnic Heritage series
General Editors: David M. Brownstone and Irene M. Franck

Facts On File
New York • Oxford

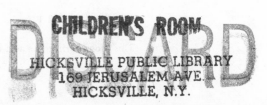

CHILDREN'S ROOM

DISCARD

HICKSVILLE PUBLIC LIBRARY
169 JERUSALEM AVE.
HICKSVILLE, N.Y.

The Irish-American Heritage

Copyright © 1989 by David M. Brownstone and Irene M. Franck

All rights reserved. No part of this book may be
reproduced or utilized in any form or by any
means, electronic or mechanical, including photo-
copying, recording, or by any information storage
and retrieval systems, without permission in
writing from the publisher. For information
contact:

Facts On File, Inc.
460 Park Avenue South
New York, New York 10016
USA

Library of Congress Cataloging-in-Publication Data

Brownstone, David M.
    The Irish-American heritage / David M. Brownstone.
      p.   cm. — (America's ethnic heritage)
    Bibliography: p.
    Includes index.
    Summary: Explores the history, culture, and contributions of Irish-
Americans from colonial times to the present day.
    ISBN 0-8160-1630-5
    1. Irish Americans—History—Juvenile literature.   [1. Irish
Americans—History.]   I. Title.   II. Series.
E184.I6B87 1989
973'.049162—dc19   88-28973

British CIP data available on request.

Facts On File books are available at special discounts when
purchased in bulk quantities for businesses, associations,
institutions, or sales promotion. Please contact the Special
Sales Department of our New York office at 212/683-2244
(dial 800/322-8755 except in NY, AK, or HI).

Text & Jacket Design by Cathy Hyman
Composition by Facts On File, Inc.
Printed in the United States of America

10 9 8 7 6 5 4 3 2 1

This book is printed on acid-free paper.

J 973.04916
B

Contents

YA
973.0416
3

Preface

The Irish-American Heritage is a volume in the *America's Ethnic Heritage* series, which explores the unique background of each of America's ethnic groups—their history and culture, their reasons for leaving home, their long journey to America, their waves of settlement in the new land, their often-difficult years of adjustment as they made their way into the American mainstream, and their contributions to the overall society we call "America."

We would like to thank the many people who helped us in completing this work: our expert typist, Mary Racette; Domenico Firmani, photo researcher *par excellence*; skilled cartographer Dale Adams; James Warren, our excellent editor at Facts On File; his very able assistant, Barbara Levine; publisher Edward Knappman, who supported the series from the start; and the many fine members of the Facts On File editorial and production staff.

We also express our special appreciation to the many librarians whose help has been indispensable in completing this work, especially to the incomparable staff of the Chappaqua Library—Director Mark Hasskarl; the reference staff, including Mary Platt, Paula Peyraud, Terry Cullen, Martha Alcott, and Carolyn Jones; Jane McKean, Caroline Chojnowski, Marcia Van Fleet, and the entire circulation staff—and the many other librarians who, through the Interlibrary Loan network, have provided us with the research tools so vital to our work.

David M. Brownstone
Irene M. Franck

America's Ethnic Heritage

The United States is a great sea of peoples. All the races, nations, and beliefs of the world are met here. We live together, joined with each other while at the same time keeping our own separate identities. And it works. Sometimes there is pain and struggle for equality and justice, but it works—and will for as long as we all want it to.

We have brought with us to America all the ethnic heritages of the world. In that respect, there is no other place like this on Earth—no other place where all the histories of all the peoples come together. Some have therefore called the United States a great "melting pot." But that is not quite right. We do not mix and completely merge our ethnic heritages. Instead we mix them, partially merge them, and at the same time keep important parts of them whole. The result is something unique called an American.

The
Irish-American
Heritage

1

The Irish Heritage

There is a broad, deep connection between Ireland and the United States. It goes back long before there was a United States, to the days when British North America was just being born. For over three and a half centuries, people from Ireland have been coming to the place that eventually became the United States. Some came as indentured servants, trading years of their freedom for passage to the new American colonies. Some came as free, prosperous people, well able to make their way in the New World. Millions came as refugees from the starvation and plague that gripped Ireland in the middle of the 19th century. Millions more came to join their friends and families in seeking opportunity in a new land, as some continue to do today.

Many Irish immigrants were Protestants, with roots in England and Scotland, as well as Ireland. Most were Catholics, with roots in Ireland going back to the earlier peoples who lived there. Among these were the early Europeans, who had been in Ireland for almost 9,000 years; Celts, who came perhaps 3,000 years ago; the Viking invaders, who swept down from the north about 1,200 years ago; and the Normans, who came after their conquest of England.

Today, there are two countries in Ireland, and what sometimes seems to be two wholly opposite peoples fighting a never-ending battle over Northern Ireland. For the purposes of this book, though, there is one land that is Ireland. It is a land that has sent millions of people to the United States, and its cultures have had deep impact on the shaping of the United States.

In a certain sense, there are at least two Irish-American heritages—the heritage of the main body of the Protestants who came in the early years of colonial America and the new American nation, and the heritage of the millions of Catholics who came in the 19th century. But there were also Catholics who came early, and Protestants who came late, and a mixing of all the people of Ireland with all the other peoples of the world in the huge, diverse mosaic that is American life. The story of Ireland, of the coming of the Irish to America, and of that joining and partial assimilation into America society is what this book is about.

The Question of Irishness

In the United States, though not in Ireland, it is customary to call Irish-American Catholics "Irish," and Irish-American Protestants "Scotch-Irish," a name that began to be widely used in the 1750s. Irish-American Protestants fully adopted the appelation "Scotch-Irish" in the 1840s. They wished to distance themselves from the hundreds of thousands of Irish Catholics beginning to arrive in the United States in the famine and plague years of the late 1840s. For their part, most Irish-American Catholics very quickly began to see and call themselves the only "real" Irish. They often denied the essential "Irishness" of the Protestants. Indeed, even today many Irish-American writers confine their work to only the Catholic Irish-American experience.

This strange development has everything to do with the long conflict in Ireland, and between Ireland and England—and hardly anything at all to do with truth, history, or the Irish-American experience and heritage. The story of Ireland and of Irish-Americans is the story of all of Ireland's peoples, in the Old World and the New. Often, it is the story of the con-

Songs of Ireland, made so popular in the early 20th century by Irish singer John McCormack, appealed to Irish-American Protestants and Catholics alike, for "Irishness" knows no political boundaries. (By E. F. Foley, 1909, Library of Congress)

flict itself, which has played such an important role in shaping the Irish people and the Irish-American heritage.

For the first two centuries in America, it was not at all that way. Those who came to America from Ireland thought of themselves—and were seen by others—as Irish, whatever their religion or origin. The Irish Protestants, usually Presbyterians, who went out to the frontier were Irish. The Irish Catholics or Protestants who arrived as indentured servants were Irish. The early Irish Catholic immigrants who became Protestants in America, as so many did, were also Irish. The prosperous Protestant English-Irish immigrants, perhaps Anglicans or Quakers, were Irish too. They were often active in forming such early societies as the Friendly Sons of St. Patrick. The Irish revolutionaries on the run to America after failed uprisings were both Protestant and Catholic.

The truth is that very few English and Scottish immigrants stayed for only a short while in Ireland and then came to America. The great majority of the Irish Protestants who went to America had been in Ireland for generations, rather than just a few years. Their reasons for emigrating from Ireland and coming to America varied. But those reasons were rooted in Irish conditions, rather than the emigrants' earlier Scottish and English origins. Whether Protestant or Catholic, whether originally Celtic, Danish, Norman, English, or Scottish, almost all of those who came to America from Ireland were undeniably Irish.

At the same time, the long Catholic-Protestant conflict and separation in Ireland meant that many of the Catholic and Protestant Irish who came to America lived in quite separate communities. And some of the deep angers and prejudices of the Old Country spilled over into the new. The history of the Catholic Irish in America was deeply affected by the bitter prejudice they encountered in British North America and then in the new United States. English-Irish and Scotch-Irish Protestant settlers formed much of the population of the English colonies in North America. And they brought with them to America tremendously strong prejudice against Irish Catholics. Early Catholic Irish immigrants faced such prejudice in the form of open discrimination and "anti-Papist"—meaning anti-Catholic—laws throughout the colonies. Those anti-Catholic laws were mostly ended by the new United States after the American Revolution, though some anti-Catholic state laws remained into the 1800s. But the prejudice behind them remained far longer, and is present to this day in some areas and in some parts of the American population. To understand the history of the Catholic Irish in America, we must take into account that strong, long-enduring prejudice. It goes back at least as far as Ireland in the 1500s, and then comes across the sea to America with the very earliest groups of English immigrants. And we must also take into account the Irish Catholic reaction to that prejudice, for it very strongly influenced the course of Irish-American history.

The Main Waves of Irish Immigration

Ireland has sent a larger proportion of its people to the United States than any other country in the world. Only Great Britain and Germany have sent more immigrants, and out of much larger populations. Well over five million Irish have come to America in the past three and a half centuries. They arrived in two main waves, followed by a steady flow of immigration that continues today. The first wave, numbering a few hundred thousand people in all, came in colonial times. It included mostly what were then called "Ulster Scots," later called "Scotch-Irish," though there were several other kinds of Irish Protestants and many Catholics as well. Some of the people of this wave settled on the Atlantic coast, but most went inland. They became some of America's earliest pioneers, starting on the way west that would centuries later bring them to the Pacific.

The second wave was over ten times larger. These were the mostly Catholic people of the great emigration out of Ireland in the 19th century. From the 1830s on, tens of thousands of people began to leave Ireland every year. That number became hundreds of thousands every year in the late 1840s and early 1850s, as plague, famine, and hard times struck Ireland. In the half century between 1840 and 1890, over 3.2 million Irish immigrants came to the United States. In the next 40 years, to 1930, well over a million more followed.

The flow of Irish immigrants to the United States became much smaller from the 1930s through the 1960s, with about 100,000 coming during that period. But it rose sharply again in the 1980s. Many of the perhaps 100,000 to 200,000 Irish immigrants in this period came as "illegals"—that is, they arrived in the United States on temporary work visas and then remained.

The Irish-American Heritage

By now, tens of millions of Americans share the Irish-American heritage. It is impossible to really tell how many Americans have people from Ireland in their family tree. The Irish immigration started long ago, families in America were large, and there was much marital mixing in America. Any of hundreds of thousands of Americans might have a Protestant or Catholic Irish-American ancestor who came over with the first wave of immigrants. Many more might have an ancestor from the huge, primarily Catholic immigration, which followed.

But beyond that, the Irish-American heritage includes the qualities the immigrants brought to America. Their heritage very early became part of the fabric of American colonial life and then of the new American nation. Among the qualities of those Irish immigrants were pride, strength, and courage. These were the qualities much needed by Celtic peoples, who long ago were pushed to the edge of Europe, and who survived to sustain their cultures for thousands of years. These were also qualities much needed—and much present—in the early settlers who pushed west in North America. And in the millions who came later, many of them penniless, to build new lives in America, often starting with only what they could earn with their bare hands.

The Irish immigrants also brought a willingness to work; and to work long and hard. The economic side of the American dream calls for that kind of work. And that is exactly what helped very many Irish immigrants to achieve material success.

They brought a great desire for freedom too. Many of the early Protestant Irish who came to America became a tremendously important part of the American Revolution. They later argued hard for a democratic United States, as did the mostly Catholic immigrants of the 1800s and 1900s. Many who came, Catholics and Protestants alike, continued to work for Irish freedom, even while they were moving into the mainstream of American life.

Irish immigrants, both Protestant and Catholic, also brought with them a strong sense of family and community life. On the American frontier, they continued to build close communities, even as frontier life made independent strength necessary for survival. In the cities, later, the closeness of family and community generated great group strength. Important as this was, it sometimes made it a little harder for Irish-Americans to move out into the wider community, to find needed education and move easily into business and the professions.

The Irish-American heritage also includes strong political and organizational skills. Many American presidents and thousands of other elected officials are evidence of those skills.

Last, and far from least, some of the greatest of America's writers and performing artists clearly show the artistic and cultural side of the Irish-American heritage.

The heritage of Ireland is that combination of qualities and skills that the people of the Old Country brought across the sea to America. To understand it best, we first need to know something of Irish history, and to that history we now turn.

Two prime examples of Irish success in America—Republican President Ronald Reagan (left, at microphone), addressing the U.S. Congress in 1981, and Thomas P. "Tip" O'Neill (behind Reagan, at right), powerful Democratic Speaker of the House, presiding over the joint Congress. (Copyright *Washington Post*; reprinted by permission of the D.C. Public Library)

2

Ireland

Oh, my Ireland of dreams,
I am with you, it seems,
And I care not for fame or renown.
Like the black sheep of old,
I'll come back to the fold,
Little town in the old County Down.

An Irish song made famous
by the singer John McCormack

For immigrants of every nationality, the Old Country has a tremendous emotional pull. For the second generation—those born in the new land—it is often much less so, as the process of adjusting to the new life in America takes hold. For the third and beyond, the pull can become strong once again, as people seek to connect their American lives and roots to the much older histories of their families and ethnic groups.

Ireland has one of the strongest pulls of all. Perhaps this stems from the long, sometimes sad history of a land and people torn apart by many hundreds of years of foreign occupation and bitter religious differences. Perhaps it is also because of the long, deep artistic and cultural history shared by all the Celtic peoples of the British Isles—by Irish, Scottish, and Welsh musicians, singers, poets, writers, and visual artists. Perhaps it is also because of a specific time in recent Irish history, during the years of the Great Potato Famine of the 1840s, when as much as half the population of the country either died of famine and the plague that came with it, or emigrated to the New World. Whatever the reasons, Ireland exerts a tremendous pull, often far beyond the first generation and into many generations of Irish-Americans afterward. That is why anyone seeking to understand Irish-Americans and their heritage must first look across the sea to Ireland.

The Land Across the Sea

Ireland is not a very big place. It is a little over 32,000 square miles, an island about the size of Maine, lying just west of Britain off the huge landmass of Eurasia. There are many smaller inhabited islands in the area as well, about 200.

Also like Maine, Ireland has a very long, irregularly shaped seacoast, full of harbors, necks of land, and long peninsulas extending out to sea. The longest straight-line distance you can travel in Ireland is 350 miles, and you are never more than 70 miles from the sea. But the seacoast is 2,200 miles long. If it were a straight line, it would run as far as the distance from America's Atlantic coast all the way out to the Rockies.

There are mountains near the sea in many parts of the country. The highest of them, Carrantuohill, in the southwest, rises to 3,400 feet above sea level. But most of Ireland is the low-lying central plain, which has for thousands of years been excellent for farming and grazing livestock. The Irish climate also helps these enterprises, for it is generally moist and cool, with few extremes. Its temperature range is about 40 to 60 degrees Fahrenheit, with adequate rain and little flooding. Ireland's climate is much influenced by the warm Gulf Stream in the Atlantic Ocean. The Gulf Stream is the reason that Ireland, like Britain and much of Western Europe, is warm, although it lies as far north as icebound Labrador in North America.

Ireland's geography, however, provides no great natural defenses. From Britain, it is an easy trip of no more than 70 miles across the Irish Sea. From Scotland, it can be as little as 10 miles across a narrow strait to Ireland. From Scandinavia, Ireland is open from the north, with many small islands serving as stepping-stones. And unlike the Appalachians in the New World, there are no natural barriers in Ireland to hinder travel. Ireland's rich farmland, openness to invasion, and closeness to its much larger and stronger British neighbors have had a great influence on the development of its history.

The People

The peoples of Eurasia have moved about, mixed, and merged for tens of thousands of years. After all, it has been physically possible, since at least the end of the last Ice Age, 15,000 to 20,000 years ago, for people to

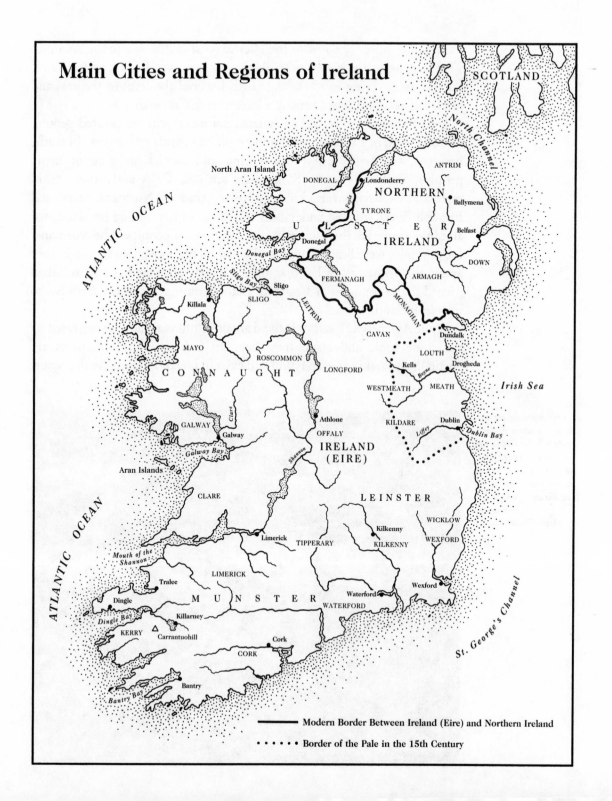

Main Cities and Regions of Ireland

walk 8,000 miles or so from the Pacific coast of Eurasia to the Atlantic. That long ago, it was even possible to walk across to Britain and Ireland, for the ice covering much of the north lowered the level of the seas and provided land bridges to many places that are now islands.

Ireland has often seemed an isolated place and with an isolated people, off on the end of Eurasia, developing without outside influences. In truth, however, the Irish reflect the mixing and partial merging of many peoples, including early Stone Age settlers, Celts and others from mainland Eurasia, several kinds of Norse invaders, Normans, Scots, and English. Even this list understates the extent of the mixing involved, for all of the above are themselves earlier mixtures of peoples. The Normans, for example, were Scandinavians who had earlier moved south into France and much of the rest of Europe, mixed mostly with the French, and then turned to the conquest of England, before coming across the Irish Sea to invade Ireland.

Stone Age people lived in Ireland about 9,000 years ago, as indicated by the stone tools and structures they left behind. The structures are particularly striking; over 1,000 still exist in Ireland. These are the "court

This beautiful eighth-century Ardagh chalice—a fine metal cup used in religious services—is an example of the Irish metalwork that has been famous for centuries.
(Irish Tourist Board)

cairns," groups of large stones, which seem to have been used for many different purposes. Some are clearly burial places, while others are thought to have been used as ceremonial sites. Some may also have been used for studying the stars and for telling time.

By 3,000 to 4,000 years ago, which was the height of the Bronze Age in Eurasia, Ireland was part of a trading network that extended from the Mediterranean to the North Sea. This was the time of the height of the ancient civilizations of Egypt, Crete, the Near East, India, and China, and of great trade and migration throughout the rest of Eurasia. In this period, Irish metalworkers were sending their work to Europe, and getting needed tin from Cornwall, in what is now southwest England. At the same time, European prospectors and traders were seeking Irish gold for export to their own metalworkers, thus adding to the mixture that was the Irish people.

The Coming of the Celts

The Celts flourished in central and eastern Europe, starting from about the fifth and sixth centuries B.C. Under pressure from other peoples, they ultimately moved west across Europe. By about 4,000 years ago, they controlled most of the Atlantic coast of present-day France, Spain, and Portugal. Their greatest sea route took them from the coast of Europe north and west to Cornwall and into the Irish Sea. This route was properly called the Celtic Seaway. Along the route they traded vitally needed Cornish tin and Spanish wine and oil for fine Irish goldwork. By about 500 B.C., Celtic art reached Ireland and at least some Celts had begun to settle there. By the time of the Roman conquest of Britain, in A.D. 43, Ireland had a substantial Celtic population. These, though, may well have been several quite different groups of Celts, rather than any kind of unified people.

With the Roman conquests of Spain and France, followed by the conquest of Britain, many more Celts came to Ireland. Gradually Ireland began to develop a unified Celtic culture. Not a unified kingdom or country, however. Ireland in this period contained hundreds of clans, each of them a little kingdom of its own. And so it stayed, for the Romans never conquered Ireland. Nor did the Germanic tribes, such as the Angles and the Saxons, who followed the Romans into England after four centuries of Roman rule. For almost a thousand years, until the Vikings came, Ireland was a Celtic land, the only untouched Celtic land left in Europe. Much of

Britain had been Celtic before the Romans came, but many Celts fled to Scotland, Wales, Cornwall, or across the English Channel back to Brittany on the European mainland when the Romans took Britain. Later, after the Germanic tribes came, only the Scottish highlands and parts of Wales and Cornwall remained Celtic. The Celts of Britain and the Celts of Ireland also spoke different Celtic dialects. There was much emigration back and forth over the narrow strait between northern Ireland and Scotland, making language differences smaller between the Scots and the Irish. Even so, from Roman times on, Ireland developed a separate Celtic land, with its own language and culture.

Christianity Comes to Ireland

Legend has it that St. Patrick drove the snakes from Ireland. Be that as it may, there is no doubt that in the 430s A.D. a Christian missionary named Patrick, probably a Celt from the British side of the Irish Sea, was a key figure in bringing Christianity to Ireland. He may not have been the

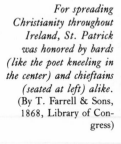

For spreading Christianity throughout Ireland, St. Patrick was honored by bards (like the poet kneeling in the center) and chieftains (seated at left) alike. (By T. Farrell & Sons, 1868, Library of Congress)

first Christian missionary in Ireland, but he was a very influential one. St. Patrick is still greatly respected as the founder of the Roman Catholic church in Ireland.

The church he and other early Irish Catholics founded had a strong streak of independence in it, perhaps part of its Celtic heritage. The Celts were a great people who had fought Rome (destroying it once in 387 B.C.) throughout western Europe, and who by then had been building their own culture in Ireland for many centuries.

This early church also reflected the Ireland of its time. The many small monasteries—that is, independent religious organizations—mirrored the family and clan organizations of the Irish Celts. The monastic orders held strong beliefs and were missionaries who often sought to take Christianity beyond Ireland. It was an adventurous time, besides, with Irish sea rovers island-hopping north and west and establishing monasteries in Scotland and on the European mainland. Some of those monasteries persist to this day.

Irish Celtic sea rovers traveled far out into the Atlantic Ocean as early as the seventh century A.D. A monk named Brendan, later St. Brendan, may have visited Iceland as early as the sixth century. He described what seems to have been a volcano in eruption, which could have been nowhere in the north Atlantic but Iceland. When the Norse Vikings reached Iceland in the ninth century, they probably saw that Irish rovers had been there before them. That was natural, for the Irish had been a seagoing people for thousands of years, and it is a short trip from each of the major northern Atlantic islands to the next one. The Shetlands lie only a little way to the north and west. The Faeroes lie only 200 miles farther northwest beyond the Shetlands. Then it is only 400 miles more to Iceland. For that matter, it is only 200 miles beyond that to Greenland, and North America. There is no conclusive evidence that the Irish rovers went west of Iceland, but they could have, as the Norse Vikings did a few hundred years later.

The Irish monk, Dicuil, wrote of the North Atlantic and its islands in A.D. 825:

> All round our land of Hibernia [Ireland] there are islands . . . . Off the coast of the island of Britain are many islands, some big, some small, some middling; some lie in the sea to the south of Britain, some to the west; but they are most numerous in the northwestern sphere and the north. On some of these islands I have lived, on others set foot, of some had a sight, of others read.

It is now thirty years since clerics who lived in that island [possibly Iceland] from the first day of February to the first day of August told me that not only at the summer solstice, but in the days on either side of it, the setting sun hides itself at the evening hour as if behind a little hill, so that no darkness occurs during that very brief period of time, but whatever task a man wishes to perform, even to picking the lice out of his shirt, he can manage it precisely as in broad daylight. And had they been on a high mountain, the sun would at no time have been hidden from them.

The Irish monks and rovers went in other directions, as well. The missionary Columba, later St. Columba, in A.D. 563 founded an important monastery on the island of Iona, off the Scottish coast, side by side with an Irish invasion of Scotland. There was an Irish Catholic kingdom in Scotland late in the sixth century. The monk, Aidan, later St. Aidan, in A.D. 635 founded the great monastery of Lindisfarne, on an island off the coast of northeastern England. Irish monks also founded monasteries in France and Switzerland during the same period.

The Vikings

A great power was to come to Ireland, starting late in the eighth century. The *Annals of Ulster*, in the northern part of Ireland, recorded the event:

The sea spewed forth floods of foreigners over Erin [Ireland], so that no haven, no landing place, no stronghold, no fort, no castle might be found but it was submerged by waves of Vikings and pirates.

In fact, the name *Viking* meant "pirate" in those times. The Vikings were actually three peoples. The Swedish Vikings, also known as the Rus, went east and south on the Russian rivers to conquer Russia and much of eastern Europe. The Danish Vikings went south along the western rivers into the heart of Europe, and west across the North Sea to conquer much of England. The Norse Vikings went south and west—south into the Irish Sea and west to Iceland and the New World.

In 793 the Vikings came out of the sea to overrun Lindisfarne. In 795, they attacked Iona. They used both as bases for what then became a series of ever-increasing attacks on the northern islands and the Irish coast. By the

After the coming of the Vikings in medieval Ireland, many church buildings were abandoned and left to fall into ruin, like these on Devenish Island. (Library of Congress)

830s, they had moved up the Irish rivers and were beginning to establish permanent bases on the Irish mainland. By the 840s, they had started what became permanent settlements on many parts of the Irish coast, including Dublin, Limerick, Wexford, and Waterford. Wave after wave of Viking invaders kept coming for 200 years. As the newcomers married into the Celtic people, there was a gradual mixing of Norse and Irish. There were Irish, for example, among the early Norse settlers of Iceland.

Some early historians made much of the Celtic King Brian Boru of Munster, the southern region of Ireland. Brian is said to have unified Ireland, and finally ended the Viking threat. But by 1014 and despite the battle of Clontarf, in which the Vikings of Dublin were defeated, the Vikings were very much a part of Irish life. Actually, after the battle and Brian's subsequent murder, Ireland once again became a land of many competing factions.

The Normans Come

The Norse Vikings never really conquered Ireland. They did take much of the seacoast, and established a Kingdom of Man and the Sudreys in the

Western Isles of Scotland, which they called their Southern Isles. But, they founded no unified kingdom that ruled over Ireland or even a large part of Ireland as did the Danes in England.

With the Danish Vikings who had gone south into Europe, the story was entirely different. These Vikings were to become the Normans, an immensely strong people who in their day conquered much of western and southern Europe. A Frenchman named Ermentarius recorded their coming in western Europe in the ninth century A.D.:

> The number of ships grows: the endless stream of Vikings never ceases to increase. Everywhere the Christians are victims of massacres, burnings, plunderings: the Vikings conquer all in their path, and no one resists them.

In 1066, the Normans took England. In 1170, the first of the Norman invaders of Ireland crossed the Irish Sea, led by Richard Fitzgilbert de Clare, called Strongbow. They began what would become seven and a half centuries of first partial and then full occupation of Ireland by English power. That occupation had enormous consequences for all Ireland and for the millions of Irish who ultimately came to America. From then on, the histories of Ireland and England were to be connected, always to the disadvantage of Ireland. Increasingly, Ireland was to come under English control, though not without centuries of battle. Increasingly, England was to take profit from Ireland, and Ireland was to become more and more an outright colony of England. In the American colonies, a single revolt in 1776 succeeded, resulting in the formation of the United States. In Ireland, so much closer to England, revolt after revolt failed, until the twentieth century.

Strongbow set himself up as king—at least in name—of Leinster, one of Ireland's four provinces. That did not suit *his* king, Henry II of England, who then made plans to invade Ireland with a strong army. Strongbow gave way without a fight. Henry came to Ireland peacefully, held court in Dublin in 1171 and 1172, and took the allegiance of kings and chiefs throughout Ireland. He left his deputy, Hugh de Lacy, in control of part of Ireland, ruling from Dublin, and recognized Irish Rory O'Connor as High King of most of the rest of Ireland.

All this only made firm the English presence in Ireland. From then on, the English expanded, in a continuing long war with the Irish, often in alliance with one or another Irish faction. By 1250, the Norman English controlled about three-quarters of Ireland.

But the Norman English did not complete their conquest of Ireland. England's Norman kings focused their attention on the wars they were fighting against the French, and their continuing wars in Wales and Scotland. The Norman invaders were strong, and the Norman castles far stronger than the Irish ring fortifications. But there were too few Normans in Ireland to completely overcome the stubborn Irish resistance. Nor could the Normans defeat a single Irish king and army and take control of the country as they had in England. The main weakness of the Irish was their lack of unity against the invader. That weakness became something of a strength in Ireland then, just as in our time guerrilla forces are able to successfully resist much stronger invading armies. For the Normans, Ireland in the late 1200s became a cost and a burden. The Norman situation in Ireland was made even more difficult when the Scots invaded northern Ireland in 1315. The invasion ultimately failed, but it greatly helped the resisting Irish to push the Normans back into much smaller areas of control, centering on Dublin.

The Irish were not able to regain all of Ireland, or even come close to doing so. English power was in Ireland to stay, and could be expanded, at least temporarily, at any time the English were willing to pour in the strength needed. That was so even later, when the Irish were able to unite, for England was always far stronger than Ireland, and very close.

What did happen was the development of two strengths and two quite different cultures in Ireland, one of them Celtic Irish and the other Norman. And with this came anger, with anger often becoming hate. The Irish regarded the English as invaders and exploiters. The English regarded the Irish as an inferior people, to be exploited and discriminated against in every possible way. Invaders throughout history have always found it easy to justify their actions by coming to believe their subject peoples were inferior. In Ireland, the resulting hatred, later made even worse by religious differences, was to haunt Irish-English attitudes and relations for seven centuries. The hatred remains even today—and in America, as well as in Europe.

The split between the two cultures extended far beyond government and warfare. One of the greatest areas of friction was religion. England was Catholic in those centuries, with the English Catholic clergy strongly connected to the Catholic Pope in Rome. But the Irish had long been more independent of Rome and were also resisting certain changes in Catholicism that occurred during the 12th century. As a result, even before the Norman invasion of Ireland, Roman Catholicism and Irish

Catholicism had been in conflict. Soon after the Norman invasion, the Pope effectively recognized their claims to Ireland. The Celtic Irish then were resisting both the Norman invasion and the Roman Catholic church. The result was a deeply split Catholic church, as well as a deeply split set of kingdoms in Ireland.

This fragmented Ireland was to exist for two more centuries. English political influence gradually became smaller as the English area of control was down to the varying area called the Pale, which sometimes extended as little as 20 miles west and 40 miles north of Dublin.

The Full Conquest of Ireland

In the early 1500s, a new era was beginning all over Europe. It was the time of the great flowering of art and culture that was called the Renaissance. The Europeans had just discovered the New World and initiated the process of exploration, invasion, and colonization of the Americas. The great nation-states of Europe, centered on strong kings and queens, had started their rise, replacing the feudal world of semi-independent baronies. In northern Europe, the religious movement that was to be called Protestantism began, accompanied by a long, complex war between the Protestant and Catholic states of Europe.

In England, the Tudor dynasty arose. Its powerful, long-ruling king, Henry VIII, broke with the pope and Roman Catholicism in 1533, bringing Protestantism to England.

As part of the same move to increased power, Henry built up English direct rule in Ireland. Until Henry VIII, the English kings had ruled through their nobility in Ireland. They had very little direct contact and therefore had little real power in Ireland. From Henry onward, English power was to come much more strongly into Ireland. From 1534 to 1535, Henry provoked a revolt of his own nobles in Ireland and then crushed it, sending his own soldiers and officials to control the Pale, the area of English control. And starting in the late 1530s, the English began to bring Protestantism to Ireland, though not yet with anything like the great religious conflicts that were to come later.

Following Henry's reign, his daughter, Mary, ruled England. Her reign lasted only five years, from 1553 to 1558. She was a Catholic, and for a little while brought Catholicism back to England and England's part of Ireland. It was during Mary's brief period of rule that the idea of

"Plantation" was implemented. *Plantation* meant, literally, the planting of English settlers into Irish areas that had been resistant to English rule. The movement took hold weakly at first, for there was strong Irish resistance. But once started it was to be carried on by other, stronger English rulers. In this period, English adventurers of many kinds also came to Ireland, settling land taken from Irish landowners.

Elizabeth I of England came to the throne in 1558. With her came what was for England a great age, the age of Shakespeare, of the destruction of the Spanish Armada, and of the triumph of Protestant England over Catholic Spain. But for Celtic and Catholic Ireland, it was a time of great disaster. Under Elizabeth I's reign, the policy of "plantation" was greatly expanded, most of it in the southern Irish province of Munster, but some in the northern province of Ulster as well. Now, too, a time of religious hatred and its accompanying massacres began.

Soon Irish resistance to English rule and "plantation" became merged with the English-Spanish wars and the all-European Protestant-Catholic

Hugh O'Neill, earl of Tyrone, in Ulster (northern Ireland), led a great Irish force against the English in Ireland in the last years before 1600.
(Library of Congress)

conflicts. From 1579 to 1581, there were risings in several parts of Ireland, accompanied by the landing of small Spanish and Italian expeditions. All were put down, sometimes with the massacres of hundreds of prisoners. The lands of the rebels were taken by the English and used to create large, new "plantations" in Munster. These drew an estimated 10,000 to 12,000 English settlers into Ireland in the late 1500s. This was far more than the migration to the new colonies in North America in that period. The "plantations" with their land grants to settlers, were to provide the pattern the English used in such North American colonies as Virginia and the Carolinas.

In 1595, war flared between the English and Irish in Ulster, which had never been successfully conquered by the English. The Irish, led by Hugh O'Neill, raised a powerful force and declared themselves allies of the Spanish in the continuing English-Spanish wars. In 1598, Ulster forces defeated a 4,000-strong English army, and O'Neill called for an all-Irish, anti-Protestant rising. His call was answered, and the Irish made attacks on English settlements throughout the country, successfully at first. But by 1600 English forces had defeated both the Irish and the small Spanish army sent to help them. From then on, even though there were risings still to come, England effectively ruled all Ireland.

The Plantation of Ulster

It was in the north, in Ulster, that the largest and most successful of the English attempts at "plantation" occurred. Ulster had been the area of strongest resistance to English rule, and the heart of the rising in 1595 to 1604. The rising had been ended by a negotiated settlement, rather than by massacres, but Hugh O'Neill and the other Ulster leaders found themselves in a dangerous position. In 1607, O'Neill and many others fled to Europe, in what was called "The Flight of the Earls." They were judged outlaws by the English, who took their land. The English then proceeded to make six of the nine counties of northern Ireland into a huge "plantation," and brought in many thousands of settlers, most from Scotland and some from England. The other three counties of northern Ireland had already been mostly taken by the English.

This plantation was not entirely successful, for many of the new English owners of large parcels of land rented them to Irish tenants, and there was continuing resistance to the English. But it was successful enough for a

Protestant, mainly Scottish, majority to emerge in northern Ireland. Later, this "Scotch-Irish" population was to supply the first major Irish emigration to the American colonies.

The Ulster plantation was "successful" in another sense, as well. This new Irish population endured. From it grew the Protestant population of Northern Ireland, the Catholic minority in Northern Ireland, and the deep divisions that to this day endure between the two. The questions faced by all the people of Northern Ireland and Ireland go back a very long way.

In Ireland, early in the 1600s, "plantation" also proceeded in many other parts of the country, though nowhere as fully as in Ulster. So did the English attempt to import Protestantism. In 1605, Protestantism was declared the state religion, and Catholicism was outlawed in Ireland. This outlawing of Catholicism was impossible to enforce, though, for English rule was not yet so strong in Celtic Catholic Ireland.

English actions against Catholicism in Ireland have always apparently had the undesired effect of actually strengthening the Irish Catholic church. As in so many other countries, an outlawed faith becomes even more attractive than before and a focus for dissent. It was certainly so in Ireland in those years.

The Time of the Massacres

But the worst was yet to come. In October 1641, rebellion again broke out in Ireland. It was particularly successful in Ulster, where it took on much the nature of a civil war between Catholics and Protestants. All over Ireland, Protestants were massacred and driven out. Many of them fled to the port cities remaining under English control and then out to England, while others continued to fight in small pockets of Protestant resistance. Charles I, then king of England, took no decisive action. Unfortunately, however, no effective Irish government emerged, for the Anglo-Irish and Celtic-Irish revolutionaries then spent eight long years arguing among themselves about whether to maintain their ties with England or seek new alliances among the Catholic nations of Europe.

The argument was ended by Oliver Cromwell. In 1648, Protestant forces in England themselves rebelled against Charles I, and he was eventually beheaded. In the summer of 1649, Cromwell led a 30,000-strong English army against Ireland, and spent most of the next year systematically reducing the country to ruin. His reconquest of Ireland for

Over the years, many thousands of people were killed in anti-Catholic massacres in Ireland, such as this one at Scullabogue. (From *History of the Irish Rebellion in 1798*)

England was accompanied by the kinds of atrocities that accompany so many religious wars, complete with widespread massacres of innocent Catholic noncombatants and the burning of large areas. He left behind a large English garrison, and a new policy that took most of the remaining Catholic property in Ireland and gave it to new Protestant landowners.

Here is Cromwell, justifying the brutal massacre of over 2,000 Irish soldiers and civilians at Drogheda, in September 1649—one of the many massacres of the time:

> I believe we put to the sword the whole number of defendants. I do not think thirty of the whole number escaped with their lives. Those that did are in safe custody for Barbados. . . . I am persuaded that this is a righteous judgement of God upon those barbarous wretches who have imbued their hands in so much innocent blood; and that it will tend to prevent the effusion of blood for the future—which are the satisfactory grounds to such actions, which otherwise cannot but work remorse and regret.

The Wild Geese

For Celtic Catholic Ireland, the new Irish world that emerged was a disaster. In Protestant Ireland, the Catholics were no more than a despairing, poverty-stricken underclass, who worked as hand-to-mouth small tenant farmers and servants, and often had no work at all. Thousands fled to the Catholic countries of Europe. Many of the men served as soldiers in the armies of the French and Spanish. These Irish soldiers were called "the wild geese," for they had "flown away" from Ireland. France had an Irish Brigade until the French Revolution of 1789. Spanish soldiers with Irish names spread all over the New World. Some, like Chile's Bernardo O'Higgins, later became revolutionaries against Spain and are great national heroes today in South America.

Many of the poorest Irish refugees came to the New World as indentured servants (who were under contract to work for a number of years) as well as other kinds of immigrants. From this group came the earliest Irish Catholics to the British North American colonies.

William and Mary

Yet the Protestant-Catholic struggle in England and in Europe was not yet over. Nor was it over in Ireland. In 1685, James II, the son of the beheaded Charles I and a strong Catholic, became the English king. Among other things, he immediately proceeded to favor the Catholic church in Ireland. His wife, Mary, had a son in 1688, who was then heir to the English throne. However, powerful English Protestants invited William of Orange, who then led the Dutch Republic, to become king of England. William came with a strong Dutch army, was welcomed by the English, and James fled the country. This was England's entirely peaceful revolution of 1688, which the English call the Glorious Revolution.

In Ireland, it brought widespread Catholic rebellion, another civil war, and yet another massacre of Protestants by Catholics. James II landed in Ireland in 1689, coming with promises of French support, to lead the revolt. But by mid-summer, English-Dutch naval forces had lifted the Catholic siege of Protestant Londonderry, in Ulster. And by the next year, William of Orange came, at the head of a large army.

During the ill-fated Irish Rebellion in 1798, the "Loyal Little Drummer" is killed by British soldiers.
(From *History of the Irish Rebellion in 1798*)

The Battle of the Boyne

On July 1, 1690, the largest battle in Irish history was fought. When it was over, so was all hope of an independent Ireland for over two more centuries. On that day, at the River Boyne, about 40 miles north of Dublin, an army of 36,000 men, led by William of Orange, met and defeated an army of 25,000 men, led by James II. The English army included English, Ulster Protestant, Dutch, German, and other Protestant troops from all over northern Europe. The Irish army included Irish Catholics, some Irish Protestants, and 7,000 French troops. Their color—perhaps in tribute to Ireland's climate—was green, and their symbol the shamrock, the green clover leaf.

A year later, English-Dutch forces destroyed the remaining Irish armies, finally taking Limerick and ending the war with the Treaty of Limerick. By the terms of the treaty, the Irish and French soldiers were allowed to leave the country. Some 12,000 of them then sailed for France. The Irish soldiers in this defeated army joined the "wild geese" already spread out all over the world. There were revolts against English rule still to come, but this was the last large battle to be fought on Irish soil, and the last truly strong rebellion until the successful battle for independence in the 20th century.

Protestant Ireland

I met with Nappur Tandy, and he took me by the hand,
And he said "How's poor old Ireland, and how does
    she stand?
"She's the most distressful country that ever yet
    was seen,
They are hanging men and women there for the
    wearing of the green!"

Then came 230 years of English rule. Soon, under the "penal laws" passed by the Protestant Irish Parliament, most of the few remaining Catholics who still owned land were either driven from their land or converted to Protestantism. The Catholic church was not officially outlawed, but severe discrimination against Catholics and the Catholic clergy became part of the law of the land. Even so, Catholicism was still practiced by the mass of the Irish Celtic people. Although it was weak and fragmented as an organized religion, it actually became stronger as a mass belief than it had been in earlier, freer times. In Ireland, with a small group of foreign Protestant occupiers holding almost all the land and wealth, and all the top positions in the land, Catholicism became the faith and shield of the poor.

Yet it did not remain as simple as that. Many Protestants soon began to regard themselves as Irish, rather than English and Scottish. And the English government soon began to discriminate against Irish Protestants, as part of English colonial policy. The same English colonial attitudes that led to trade discrimination against the American colonies and helped begin the American Revolution, were at work in Ireland even earlier. There was English discrimination against Ireland's growing woolen industry, which all but destroyed it, and encouraged thousands of Protestants to emigrate to the New World from Ulster. There were rent increases for farmed land, as English owners took more and more profit from an Ireland that could ill afford to pay. In colonial Ireland, Protestant movements against English rule soon developed. Later, many Protestants would join the Catholic majority in fighting for an independent Ireland. Not all; by no means all. Hatred often broke out into armed, local conflicts. These continued to plague Catholic-Protestant relations in Ireland, as they do in Northern Ireland to this day. But from the 1790s on, there was a joint Protestant-Catholic effort to free Ireland.

Rebellion Again

The American and French revolutions brought tremendous new ideas, and with them tremendous changes throughout Europe and the Atlantic world. During the American Revolution, England was forced to relax its hold on Ireland somewhat. In that period the Irish Parliament passed the first of what would become a long series of laws easing discrimination against Catholics. When France and England went to war, in 1779, England further eased restrictions on Protestant Ireland, as well, among other things making the Irish Parliament and courts independent. And when revolution came to France, in 1789, England became worried enough about Ireland to push through a group of laws removing many of the century-old discriminations against Irish Catholics. By 1793, Irish Catholics had the right to vote, bear arms, own land, practice law, establish their own schools, marry Protestants, and hold all but the highest offices.

Many discriminatory laws and practices remained, however. And successful revolutions, even though elsewhere, very often encourage people making gains to want more. That is what in our time has come to be called the "crisis of rising expectations." It was so in Ireland in the 1790s, as well. By 1798, an alliance of Irish Catholics and Protestants, led by Protestant Wolfe Tone, had formed into the Society of United Irishmen. The society called for far more than the English were willing to give, including complete religious and political equality, along American and French lines.

In 1796, Tone sailed from France with a French fleet and 30,000 men, set for an invasion that would trigger rebellion all over Ireland. But in history, and especially maritime history, accidents caused by nature do happen. The Great Spanish Armada that set out to take England in the time of Elizabeth I was defeated as much by bad weather as by the English fleet. The great Mongol fleet that set out to take Japan in the time of Kublai Khan was utterly destroyed by storms in the Sea of Japan. In this case, the French fleet that set out to invade Ireland became lost in the fogs of the

Wolfe Tone, a Protestant, led the Society of United Irishmen, including both Irish Catholics and Protestants, in the fight against the British. (Library of Congress)

North Atlantic. When half the fleet did not show up for the landing, the French withdrew.

Two years later, in 1798, Tone's Irish revolt came, but only as a series of small rebellions throughout the country. Nor were the rebels united, for in many places Irish Catholics fought Irish Protestants far harder than either fought the English. The 40,000 British soldiers put down the risings easily, though with great bloodshed. In 1800, the British forced the merger of the Irish Parliament into the British Parliament, by the Act of Union. The dream of a free Ireland was far from dead, but freedom for even part of Ireland was not to come for another 120 years.

The Catholic Emigrants' Ireland

The Ireland from which millions of Catholic emigrants would come to America was the Ireland of the 19th century. This was an Ireland of a con-

Farmers whose crops had failed could no longer pay their rent and so were evicted by government officials, despite their pleas for mercy.
(Author's archives)

tinuing battle for freedom from British domination. It saw a long series of British moves to meet Irish demands, while still holding Ireland for Britain. In this Ireland, the battle for freedom was carried on mainly through mass meetings and peaceful demands, rather than by armed rebellion, although there was much violence and the threat of rebellion was always present. There were still risings, such as Robert Emmet's rising in Dublin, in 1803. But this was nothing like the time of risings and civil wars that Ireland had come through since Henry VIII's decision to directly rule Ireland almost two and a half centuries earlier.

Nineteenth-century Ireland was also the time of a wholly revived Irish Catholic church, now entirely out from underground. This Catholic church was no longer poor, persecuted, and a champion of the cause of revolution. Far from it. This was a Catholic church much concerned about the threat of revolutionary France and its persecution of all churches and clergy. The British and the Irish Protestant and Catholic landlords and officials could and did live very easily with this Catholic church. Irish revolutionaries found living with it far more difficult.

In 1823, Irish Catholic lawyer Daniel O'Connell began what soon became a huge movement to achieve full equality for Irish Catholics. At that time, Catholics were barred from representing Ireland in the British House of Commons. O'Connell's chief demand was that Catholics be admitted as representatives there. Six years later he attained a partial victory. He then turned to the great cause of the rest of his life, repeal of the Act of Union, which would bring an independent Ireland. He died without seeing it won, but his work was taken up by others. The most notable of his successors was Protestant Charles Stewart Parnell, leader of the Home Rule party later in the century, and an outstanding leader of the Irish National Land League. In the late 1870s, the National Land League fought against evictions and rent increases throughout Ireland. For O'Connell and the other reformers of his day, Ireland was a land of great promise, and the aim of Irish independence very possible to achieve.

Early 19th-century Ireland was also a land of great population, and of the potato, which was the chief means of feeding that population. These two factors, together with the continuing poverty of the great mass of Irish Catholics, were to bring about the greatest catastrophe in Irish history.

Famine and Plague

It is hard to know just how much the Irish population grew from the middle 1600s to the middle 1800s, but it clearly grew enormously. The figures available, which may be greatly understated, show that between 1690 and 1840, a period of 150 years, the Irish population grew fourfold. In 1690, there were an estimated two million people in Ireland. The Irish census of 1841 showed a population of almost 8,200,000 people, and some estimates go as high as almost 10 million. Ireland is a small country, with a good deal of it taken up by hilly and mountainous land that yields very little food. By 1841, Ireland was also one of the most densely populated countries in the world.

The great majority of the Irish were very poor, except for the small fringe of landlords and officials living on top of the large numbers of Celtic Catholic poor. Although Irish farm produce continued to increase, the differences between rich and poor were enormous, with the rich taking whatever profits there were to be had, and often taking their money out of the country. Very many landlords lived well in Britain on the income from their Irish holdings. In addition, health care was very nearly nonexistent for the poor.

The great staple food that fed the poor Irish population was the potato. The potato had been brought from the New World to Ireland and all Europe in the late 1500s. It is highly nutritious and was easy to cultivate on the small plots of land held by poor Irish tenant farmers. Compared to the other crops that could be grown in Ireland, the potato was by far the cheapest way for poor people to grow enough food to be able to feed themselves. The huge Irish population growth of those times happened for many reasons, but it clearly could not have gone nearly as far as it did without potato growing. That was so in several other countries, as well, notably Germany.

What caused disaster in Ireland between 1845 and 1849 was that the potato crop failed, because of a potato disease that first appeared in North America and later reached Europe. The European potato crop was first hit in 1845, but failed mainly in 1846, so much so that there were very few seed potatoes for the crop of 1847. The potato crop began to come back in 1848, and was mostly back by 1849, but by then the damage had been done, and it was enormous.

A poor Irish population, living on potatoes at just about a subsistence level, was hit hard by what came to be called the Great Potato Famine. Pitifully small British efforts at relief were totally inadequate to meet the needs of millions of starving people, especially as landowners continued to export food out of Ireland, all during the famine. Lady Wilde, mother of Irish playwright Oscar Wilde, described the scene in her poem, *The Famine Year*:

> There's a proud array of soldiers—what do they
>   round your door?
> They guard our masters' granaries from the thin
>   hands of the poor.
> Pale mothers, wherefore weeping?—"Would to God
>   that we were dead—
> Our children swoon before us, and we cannot give
>   them bread!"

In all, tens and perhaps hundreds of thousands starved to death.

Much worse than that, multiple plagues came along with the famine. Many people were weakened by hunger and out on the roads begging for food. It was very easy to fall prey to epidemic diseases. The Irish health care system for the poor was almost nonexistent to start with. As plague struck, the few medical people available were quickly overwhelmed, many of them also falling victim to disease. Ireland suffered a huge typhus epidemic in 1847. At the same time, it suffered a plague of relapsing fever, a plague of dysentery, and a tremendous number of cases of scurvy, as well as many kinds of other ills connected with starvation and multiple epidemics. The period is properly called the Great Famine and Plague, for perhaps 10 times as many people died of plague as died directly of starvation. No one knows just how many people died, but the best estimates are that 1 to 1.5 million people died of famine and plague in those years.

The Great Migration

Many Irish died; many also fled. As many as half a million emigrated to Britain seeking to find some sort of work and escape the plague. Some 300,000 to 350,000 emigrated to Canada, then British North America. And from 1847 through 1854, a full 1.3 million Irish emigrants went to the United States. That was about one-third of all those who came to America in those years.

Not all of this enormous emigration out of Ireland was directly caused by the famine and plague. Adding to their plight during and after the famine and plague years, many hundreds of thousands of poor Irish tenants were evicted from their land for nonpayment of rent. That is why the American Irish immigration was actually largest after, rather than during, the famine and plague.

Nor did the Irish immigration to America stop when the plagues, famine, and evictions ended. It would never again average 130,000 people a year, as it did from 1847 to 1854. But a large and steady stream of Irish immigrants came in the following decades. From 1855 to the beginning of World War I, in 1914, over 2.5 million more Irish immigrants came to America, an average of well over 40,000 Irish immigrants a year.

In all, over 5 million Irish immigrants have come to the United States. Why they came, from the earliest Protestant and Catholic settlers to the huge mass of later mainly Catholic immigrants, is the topic of the next chapter.

3

Why They Came to America

With my bundle on my shoulder,
Sure, there's no man could be bolder,
I'm leavin' dear old Ireland without warning;
For I lately took the notion for to cross the
briny ocean,
And I'm off to Philadelphia in the mornin'.

During the 1600s, most of the Irish emigrants to North America were poor Celtic Catholics. A few of the more prosperous Anglo-Irish Catholic descendants of the Norman invaders came as well. Some Irish Protestants also emigrated to America in that time, most of them people of the earlier English "plantations."

Starting in the late 1600s, many more Protestants than Catholics began to emigrate. Most of these were from Ulster, in northern Ireland. All during the 1700s and into the 1830s, a large Protestant emigration out of Ulster to America continued. Much smaller numbers of Catholics continued to come to America as well.

Then, starting in the 1830s and swelling into a truly massive emigration with the potato famine and plague years of the 1840s, came the huge Irish Catholic emigration to the United States. The flow of migration continued strongly through the early decades of this century.

Ultimately, Irish immigrants of every belief and walk of life came to America. There were Catholics, Quakers, Anglicans, Presbyterians, even some German Protestants who had settled in Ireland for generations before many of them moved on to America. There were poor Protestant and Catholic indentured servants, independent farmers and artisans, the poor second sons of former Irish noble families, "wild geese" who had fled to Europe and eventually found their way to America, Protestant clerics, Catholic priests, the old, the young, and those in the prime of life. Eventually, their descendants were to form Irish-American communities well over five times as large as the whole population of Ireland.

The Earliest Irish Immigrants

As would be so for centuries, the earliest Irish immigrants came from a wide variety of backgrounds. During the 1600s, an estimated 30,000 to 75,000 Irish immigrants came to the colonies that would later become the United States. That is only a rough estimate, for good records were not kept of this migration.

The Catholics who came in those early years were mostly poor, and they emigrated as servants. Even before Oliver Cromwell's bloody Irish campaign of 1649, Ireland was a hard place for poor Catholics to make a living. Many sought a better life in America, and were willing to give years of servitude in return for a new start. Most Irish Catholic immigrants went to the West Indies in this early period, but substantial numbers also went to the mainland colonies that would later become the United States. They went to all the mainland colonies, but in largest numbers to the tobacco-growing regions of Maryland and the rich plantation country of Virginia. Some thousands of indentured servants, mainly

These two drawings highlight the contrast between the poor Irish emigrant leaving for America, and the same man as a prosperous Irish-American returning home for a visit. (Author's archives)

COMING TO AMERICA   RETURNING FOR A VISIT

THE OLD WORLD AND THE NEW

Catholic, came to America as convicts, trading prison terms for as long as 14 years of indentured near-slavery.

Many early Irish Protestant immigrants also arrived in America as servants. The basic arrangement, for poor Catholics and Protestants alike, was to sign agreements to become indentured servants. Such agreements provided that the immigrant would be bound over by law as a servant for a period of time often amounting to seven years, or even longer. During that period, the immigrant was forced by law to work long and hard as little better than a slave for the indenture holder. In return, the immigrant received passage to America and often as small cash payment after the long years were over.

However, not all who came to America as servants were bound to hard-and-fast indenture contracts. Many came as "redemptioners," meaning that they could buy back—that is, redeem—their contracts after arrival in the New World. Large numbers of Irish immigrants did just that, often borrowing money from families and friends who had come earlier.

Not all of the Irish Catholics who came in colonial days were poor servants. Some of the "wild geese" who fled English rule to become soldiers in other armies eventually found their way to North America. So did some of the dispossessed Irish Catholic landowners and other gentry in those days. Many of them were young men. America was for centuries the destination of the younger sons of well-to-do families, who could not inherit much at home and came to America to try to make their fortune. One such relatively prosperous Irish immigrant was Charles O'Carroll of Tipperary, whose grandson was a signer of the Declaration of Independence. Irish immigrant Thomas Burke eventually became governor of North Carolina.

Many of the Irish Catholics who came to America in colonial times converted to Protestantism, and so merged into the general English-speaking population of the colonies. At the time of the American Revolution, there were still only about 25,000 practicing Catholics in the new United States, although by then far more Catholics than that had arrived from Ireland alone, and many had lived long enough to create large families in the new country. But given the discriminatory laws and attitudes of the time, few Irish Catholic communities existed in the newly formed United States. In those early centuries, most Irish Catholics came to America alone. They came as servants, whether originally convicts or free people. Or they came as fare-paying passengers on their own, whether "wild geese" or second sons without inheritances. What they did not do was come as part of a mass

The success of immigrants like Thomas Burke, who became governor of North Carolina in the new United States, attracted many other Irish people to the New World.
(Library of Congress)

migration, resulting from formation of a series of immigrant chains that would bring large numbers of Catholic emigrants to the United States. That was to come later. Before the great mass of Irish Catholics came, hundreds of thousands of Irish Protestants would come to America, in just that way, and for very good reasons.

The Irish Protestants

During the 1700s, right up to the time of the American Revolution, much larger numbers of Irish immigrants came to the British colonies that were soon to become the United States. The main body of these immigrants were Protestants, and most of these were from Ulster, in northern Ireland. From the 1690s to the outbreak of the American Revolution in 1775, an estimated 200,000 Irish Protestants emigrated to America. Most went to the 13 colonies and a much smaller number to what would later become Canada. That was a very large emigration out of a total

Irish Protestant population of no more than 600,000. In fact, it amounted to somewhere between one-quarter and one-third of the Protestant population of Ireland in that period. For that many people to leave, and all for one place, there had to be very powerful pushes out of Ireland and equally strong pulls to the New World.

There were indeed a whole series of good reasons to leave Ireland. For the northern Presbyterian Protestants, who made up by far the largest part of the Protestant emigration, both religious discrimination and economic hardship were strong factors. Although they were Protestants, and less discriminated against than Catholics in Ireland, they were Dissenters. Their kind of Protestantism—Presbyterianism—was different from that of the dominant English Protestants. And although many of them could make better livings than most of the Catholic Irish, England still treated Ireland much like a colony, with profits being taken out and not put back into the country by absentee landlords. There were also unfair trade restrictions, much like those that helped cause the American Revolution.

Economic reasons were also powerful for many Anglican Protestants from all over Ireland, even though their religion was that of the dominant English. Every raise in land rent imposed by absentee landlords, every bad harvest, every new trade discrimination provided new reasons for seeking opportunity in the New World.

The relatively small numbers of Irish Quakers also encountered religious discrimination in Ireland, and they shared some of the same economic problems. An estimated 3,000 of them eventually made their way to the New World, most to the Quaker settlements started by William Penn in Pennsylvania. Penn's Irish secretary, James Logan, started the migration by making it clear that Irish Quakers would be very welcome. Once the process was started, it grew, as immigrant chains do, and a small but steady stream of Irish Quakers began to flow to America.

There were also incentives provided by American landowners and colonial governments, eager to bring new hardworking immigrants to the colonies. During the 1600s and 1700s, many colonies, including Pennsylvania, Virginia, Georgia, Maryland, and South Carolina, offered immigrants such incentives as small cash payments, inexpensive passage, low-cost land, and other help in getting started.

Landowners, too, provided such incentives to immigrants. There was much land speculation in the colonies, with landowners buying large tracts for very little, attracting new settlers with promises and incentives, and then reselling the land at large profits.

Shipping companies also successfully pulled settlers from Ireland to the New World. Company agents were eager to sell passages on their ships, which very often carried goods from America to Europe, and had much less to carry back. The immigrant trade was a profitable one, so shipowners added their own promises and incentives to attract America-bound passengers.

Although there were many negative factors pushing people out of Ireland, and many incentives and promises pulling people to America, the main reason that drew new immigrants was the truth of the promise of America. This was so for Irish Catholics even before the American Revolution, and in spite of anti-Catholic discrimination in the colonies. It was even more so for Irish Protestants of all kinds. For them, the colonies provided a combination of economic opportunity and religious freedom that was far better than anything they could expect in Ireland.

Of the many that came, some prospered, and were more free than they had been in the Old Country. As did so many immigrants from many lands they wrote "America letters" home, often sending money and urging others to come. Many who had come alone, as indentured servants or redemptioners, wrote and sent money to bring over the rest of their families. In sum, for the Irish Protestants the classic "immigrant chains" started. As with every other large American ethnic group, the establishment of these immigrant chains brought mass immigration. It was happening in the 1600s and 1700s, with other peoples from the British Isles—the English, Scottish, and Welsh. It would happen later with many of the scores of huge immigrant ethnic groups that were drawn to America—the Germans, Scandinavians, Jews, Italians, Chinese, Japanese, Poles, and all the rest. And it was to happen with the Catholic Irish in the next wave of Irish immigration, that of the 1800s.

Here is an example of the kind of "America letter" that encouraged the Irish to come to America. It was written in 1850, as a letter to the London *Times*.

> I am exceedingly well pleased at coming to this land of plenty. On arrival I purchased 120 acres of land at £1 [1 pound, about $5] an acre. . . . You must bear in mind that I have purchased the land out, and it is to me and mine an "estate for ever," without a landlord, an agent or tax-gatherer to trouble me. I would advise all my friends to quit Ireland—the country most dear to me; as long as they remain in it they will be in bondage and misery. What you labour for is

sweetened by contentment and happiness; there is no failure in the potato crop, and you can grow . . . every crop you wish. . . . I shudder when I think that starvation prevails to such an extent in poor Ireland. After supplying the entire population of America, there would still be as much corn [grain] and provisions left as would supply the world, for there is no limit to cultivation or end to land. Here the meanest laborer has beef and mutton, with bread, bacon, tea, coffee, sugar and even pies, the whole year round—every day here is as good as Christmas-day in Ireland.

The Main Wave

During the American Revolution, Irish emigration to the United States very nearly stopped. It resumed again after the Revolution, but was still rather small. That was partly because in the new, free United States, most indenture contracts were no longer recognized. The main reason, however, was that France and England were at war for almost all of the years between 1793 and the end of the Napoleonic Wars in 1814. In those years, the North Atlantic was scarcely a safe place to be. Most Irish immigrants who might otherwise have come to the New World did not do so. Some, however, chose to brave the danger. Most of them were Presbyterians from Ulster, continuing to travel in the "immigrant chains" that, by then, stretched between Ireland and America.

Ireland's economic problems continued. The few economic advances that were made were more than outweighed by a fast-increasing population. The new United States promised far more economic opportunity than the colonies ever had, as Americans spilled out through the Appalachians west toward the Mississippi. And the new country now clearly provided far more freedom than any other English-speaking land.

After the end of the Napoleonic Wars, not only was the North Atlantic safe again, but transatlantic fares came down. The same good reasons to leave Ireland for America were in place, as were the immigrant chains. In that set of conditions, full-scale Protestant emigration from Ireland resumed and grew even more.

For Irish Catholics, North America was not so very attractive during colonial times, for anti-Catholic bigotry ran high. For those who were poor, it was also hard to find the money to pay for passage. Nor were there Irish Catholic immigrant chains in existence to any great degree. Someone

Among the starving, plague-stricken Irish poor, sometimes there were more deaths than there were coffins, as here in County Cork, in the dreadful winter of 1846-1847.
(Illustrated London News)

coming to America as a redemptioner, then, might not be able to borrow enough to buy back an indenture contract.

After the American Revolution, though, several kinds of changes began to occur, which together made leaving Ireland for America a much more attractive idea for Catholics. One of the most important of these was the Revolution itself. That did not do away with anti-Catholic bigotry, but did provide a Constitution and Bill of Rights that outlawed religious discrimination. Some of the more conservative forces in the Irish Catholic church and elsewhere in Irish society did not believe in the kind of equality that the United States provided, but many poor Irish—both Catholic and Protestant—thought the new equality a very good thing indeed.

It also became cheaper and easier to cross the Atlantic, as ships became bigger, trade greatly increased, and then as steam power replaced sail power on the North Atlantic and the other oceans of the world. For millions of poor Irish, it was impossible to find 5 to 6 pounds, for that was a huge sum for the very poor in those days. But it was not impossible to find 1 to 2 pounds, to buy passage in an American "timber ship"—that is, one that had brought timber to Europe from America and would otherwise go home empty.

There was also more hope in Catholic Ireland as the 1800s unfolded. Increasing problems of overpopulation and continuing economic troubles continued to exist, but the beginning of new mass movements for Irish freedom began to be born. The English were responding by making concessions and abolishing anti-Catholic laws. When people who have had little freedom get some freedom, they begin to hope again, and they soon want more—a process that occurred in Ireland all through the early decades of the 1800s. Many stayed and hoped and worked for change in Ireland, even during repeated economic troubles. Others began to translate their new hopes into a move to America. For the first time Irish Catholic immigrant chains began to develop between Catholics in Ireland and new Irish Catholic communities in the United States and Canada.

Even before the famine and plague years, Irish Catholic emigration to the United States had grown as large as, or even a little larger than, the

Leaving home with their few goods packed on a horse-drawn cart, these Irish emigrants received the priest's blessing for their journey and headed for the nearest port, in this case Cork, where they found boats bound for New York and Quebec.
(Author's archives)

Protestant emigration. By the time the famine and plague struck, the idea of America had been firmly planted, and the means of accomplishing emigration were available. In those years, the reasons for leaving Ireland for America became simply and absolutely compelling. People fled Ireland to save their lives.

After the famine and plague years, the Irish kept right on coming, now to join millions of other new Irish-Americans who were already in place in the new land. Irish political conditions did improve somewhat from the 1800s to the 1900s, but economic conditions for the poor in Ireland continued to push people out to the promise of America. Some of those reasons persist even today, for now a new Irish emigration has begun, this one composed of the young, well-educated people who feel they can do much better in the United States than in modern Ireland.

4

Across the Sea to America

The North Atlantic, one of the world's stormiest seas, is also one of the greatest travel and trade routes. For it is the shortest way from Europe to North America.

In early times, before Columbus and the other European explorers of his day, Irish and Viking explorers moved out across the Atlantic to Iceland. Later, Vikings moving west from Iceland reached Greenland and then the mainland of North America. This far northern route took advantage of favorable east-to-west currents and then a north-to-south current along the coast of North America. But that was in relatively warm times, when ice floes did not choke the northern shipping lanes.

By the late 1400s, the far northern routes were blocked by ice, making it necessary to take open routes across the Atlantic. Going directly across the North Atlantic from Europe to North America that way is extremely hard in a sailing ship. When ships are forced somewhat south, into the open water routes, they must sail west to America against a powerful west-to-east current *and* prevailing winds from the west to the east.

That powerful current is the Gulf Stream, a great circular "river in the sea." It moves south in the Atlantic Ocean along the coasts of Europe and Africa, and then, off North Africa, swings west across the Atlantic to the Gulf of Mexico. Then it swings north somewhat off the Atlantic coast of North America, and near New England returns to Europe into the Irish Sea and the English Channel. Those taking the far northern route, as did the Irish sea rovers and the Vikings, swing north of the Gulf Stream on their way to America, and come back across open water to the north, with the current and a west wind at their backs. But those traveling west to America from Ireland and Britain, as did millions of Irish and tens of millions of other immigrants from Europe to America, were going against wind and current the whole way.

That alone made the trip to America very difficult indeed, in the days of sailing ships. By modern standards, the ships were small, and in even the best of conditions could be counted on to heave and pitch as they bucked the wind and current that ran against them. The Europe-to-America voyage, which now takes a few hours by air and five or six days in a modern, stable ocean liner, in those days often took as long as ten weeks.

But although wind, weather, and current made the trip difficult, it was humankind that made it sometimes almost impossible. For the immigrant ships were, in many periods, also crowded, unsanitary, and prone to epidemic diseases. Immigrants were crowded into "steerage," the unventilated upper holds of the immigrant ships, near the steering mechanism. There they were fed inadequately, usually had far too little fresh water, and all too often fell ill, with little or no medical help available. Very often, and especially during the famine and plague years, immigrants had only what they themselves brought on board to eat, and fresh water had to be rationed long before the ships reached America.

In periods of mass illness, as during the Irish famine and plague years, those on the immigrant ships paid a terrible price for their passage. In 1847, over 15,000 of the 90,000 immigrants who sailed from Liverpool to Quebec died on the way, or soon after in Canadian hospitals, of typhus, cholera, and other illnesses that were at that time raging unchecked in Ireland.

Here's one account of the journey that year:

Before the emigrant has been a week at sea he is an altered man. How can it be otherwise? Hundreds of poor people, men, women, and

Nineteenth-century emigrant ships were grossly overloaded, and living conditions in the cargo hold called "steerage" were primitive at best.
(Author's archives)

children of all ages, from the drivelling idiot of ninety to the babe just born, huddled together without light, without air, wallowing in filth and breathing a fetid atmosphere, sick in body, dispirited in heart, the fever patients lying between the sound, in sleeping places so narrow as almost to deny them the power of indulging, by a change of position, the natural restlessness of the disease; by their ravings disturbing those around, and predisposing them, through the effects of the imagination, to imbibe the contagion; living without food or medicine, except as administered by the hand of casual charity, dying without the voice of spiritual consolation, and buried in the deep without the rites of the Church.

The food is generally ill-selected and seldom sufficiently cooked, in consequence of the insufficiency and bad construction of the cooking places. The supply of water, hardly enough for cooking and drinking, does not allow washing. In many ships the filthy beds, teeming with all abominations, are never required to be brought on deck and aired; the narrow space between the sleeping berths and the piles of boxes is never washed or scraped, but breathes up a damp and fetid stench.

The meat was of the worst quality. The supply of water shipped on board was abundant, but the quantity served out to the passengers was so scanty that they were frequently obliged to throw overboard their salt provisions and rice . . . because they had not water enough for the necessary cooking and the satisfying of their raging thirst afterwards. They could only afford water for washing by withdrawing it from cooking of their food. I have known persons to remain for days together in their dark, close berths because they suffered less from hunger.

Immigrants as Cargo

It is not surprising that these immigrants were carried in the cargo holds called "steerage." By the mid-1800s it had been an established pattern in the trade to America for well over 200 years.

The reason for it was because, for hundreds of years, North American ships carried far more goods *to* Europe than *from* Europe. American and Canadian ships carried to Europe tobacco, cotton, timber, furs, deerskins, flax, seeds, and a score of other raw materials and partly finished goods. European ships carried back finished goods, like clothing and tools, that took up far less space in the holds of the trading ships. America-bound shippers, therefore, from the first sought additional cargo, and found it—in the form of people.

That search for westbound cargo was part of the basis for the infamous Triangle Trade, which is another way of saying the slave trade. Slave-trading ships would follow the course of the Gulf Stream, moving south from Europe to pick up slaves in West Africa, crossing the Atlantic by the southern route, delivering slaves, and then moving north up the American coast, picking up cargo that they then took back to Europe. This highly profitable trade, which enriched so many British and New England shippers, was finally stopped by order of the British government in the early 1800s. After it was stopped, shippers had to concentrate even more on getting immigrant cargoes for their ships. But much earlier, and side-by-side with the slave trade, a profitable immigrant-carrying business had been developed by transatlantic shippers.

As early as the 1620s, about the time the Pilgrims came to New England, ships sailing between Ireland and North America were carrying Irish immigrants to the Caribbean and to the southern mainland colonies, such as Virginia and Maryland. As the slave trade developed, though, there were fewer immigrant jobs available in the Caribbean, and most Irish immigrants then went to the mainland colonies.

By the mid-1700s, the large, early Protestant Irish immigration was

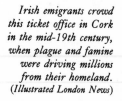

Irish emigrants crowd this ticket office in Cork in the mid-19th century, when plague and famine were driving millions from their homeland. (Illustrated London News)

well under way. From such American mid-Atlantic ports as Philadelphia, Baltimore, and New York came flax and cotton for northern Ireland's large textiles trade. Returning, the same ships carried large numbers of Irish immigrants. Some stayed to build their lives in the cities, and many more headed for the interior to claim land on the frontier. The same ships carried smaller numbers of Irish Catholics, as well, some prosperous, but most indentured servants. Many of the Irish Catholics who came to America in the years before the main Catholic immigration were later to merge into the main Protestant Irish stream, often changing their religions and sometimes their names as well.

Irish immigrants in these times also went north, to Canada. Many went to Newfoundland, on fishing boats. Some of these later found their way south into the United States, as did so many of the Irish who later came to Canada.

Timber, Cotton, and Immigrants

During the early 1800s, a large timber trade developed between Canada and Ireland. Soon, an equally large trade in Irish immigrants to Canada developed, for transatlantic fares from Ireland to Canada on the returning timber ships dropped sharply. That sharp decrease in fares was partly because of British government subsidies—that is, amounts paid to shippers directly or indirectly aimed at keeping fares low and encouraging the Irish to migrate to Canada. In the 1815 to 1820 period, fares to the United States from such Irish ports as Belfast and Londonderry, and from Liverpool, England, ran about 7 to 10 pounds each. First-class fares on the best and fastest boats cost much more. Yet soon after, in the 1830s and 1840s, fares from Ireland and England to Quebec cost only a little over 2 pounds, with fares to Canada's coastal areas costing even less. By then, the lowest fares to the United States also had come down sharply, to as little as 4 pounds, but that was still twice as much as the least expensive Canadian fares. And every pound made an enormous difference to desperately poor Irish laborers fleeing first Irish poverty and then the famine and plague.

That difference in transatlantic passage cost was the most important single reason for the way Irish Catholics moved into New England in the early 1800s. Tens of thousands of poor Irish crossed to Quebec, while thousands more went to the even closer Canadian coastal areas—now the Maritime Provinces. From there, many moved south, some by ship along the coast and others inland, south through Maine, following whatever jobs were available. Many of these early Irish immigrants formed small communities, today the centers of many of the large Irish-American communities scattered throughout New England.

In England, after the Napoleonic Wars ended in 1814, a huge textile industry developed—and with it an equally huge American cotton industry, for England's textile mills used enormous quantities of American cotton. By the 1830s, American ships were carrying large amounts of cotton to Liverpool, and carrying back large numbers of immigrants, most of them Irish. In this period, the main United States-bound immigrant ships sailed from Liverpool, although the timber ships continued to sail from Irish ports. Later in the century, United States-bound ships would once again sail directly from Irish ports. But during the peak years of the Irish-United States immigration, Irish immigrants had to travel across the Irish Sea to Liverpool, wait for ships there, and then cross the Atlantic to the United States.

Those sailing to the United States from Ireland had always been the prey of passage brokers, agents, shipowners, and ship's officers, all determined to make as much money as they could from the immigrants. Immigrant accounts of the journey are full of descriptions of how false promises lured the unwary onto leaky old ships in Irish ports, starting on nightmare journeys to America. The inexpensive timber boats were the worst, but even on the faster, more modern packet boats—which sailed on regular schedules—sailing to America often meant enduring terrible conditions, for steerage passengers.

Liverpool was even worse, especially for the poorer Irish immigrants—and most especially during the famine and plague years. To get to Liverpool, Irish immigrants had to travel to Dublin and other ports on the Irish Sea. They then crossed to Liverpool, usually crammed together on the open decks of boats made to carry a small fraction of their number. These were often cattle boats, with the cattle protected in the cargo holds, while the people up on deck had no protection from wind and weather. Some immigrants from Ireland felt that the short passage from Ireland to Liverpool was the worst part of the journey.

Arriving in Liverpool, Irish immigrants faced many hazards. There were agents and brokers ready to sell tickets to nonexistent boats. There were provisions sellers and lodging-house keepers, ready to sell food and shelter at inflated prices—some immigrants often had to wait for days or even weeks at Liverpool for boats to take them to America. The hazards should not be overstated, though. There were also some honest British government agents, some honest agents and brokers, and some honest ship's captains. The trick was to distinguish the good from the bad, in what for most Irish was a huge city and a strange country. In fact, some were so badly cheated that they lost their passage money, never made it to America, and joined the hundreds of thousands of other Irish who made their way, as best they could, in Britain in those times. But hundreds of thousands, and then millions, did cross the Irish Sea, where they joined millions of others from northern Europe on the journey to America.

The Ships

The sailing ships that carried the Irish and other immigrants across the North Atlantic were small by modern standards. Even in their own day, they tended to be smaller than the Spanish galleons, Dutch East Indiamen, and Yankee clippers. They were strongly built, to withstand the Atlantic storms they would encounter, and generally well sailed by their American, Canadian, and British crews—except when greedy shipowners and captains tried to make too much profit by overloading and failing to maintain their ships.

Later, North Atlantic sailing ships called "packets" appeared. They were strongly-built, square-rigged ships that rode fairly high in the water, even when fully loaded. By the 1820s, as the main, later wave of Irish immigration began, packet ships in the 1,000-ton range dominated the North Atlantic trade. It was in ships like these that millions of Irish and other immigrants came across the North Atlantic to America, with perhaps 1,000 people crowded into steerage on a typical trip.

In the days of sailing ships many of these trips were dangerous. Even before and after the main famine and plague years, disease was a constant threat, as were the shipboard fires and the icebergs of the North Atlantic. Historian Terry Coleman reports that between 1847 and 1853 alone, 59 emigrant ships were lost in the North Atlantic.

Yet only a few years later, it had all changed. What happened was the coming of steamships to the seas of the world. Nowhere was that more important than on the North Atlantic. As early as 1818, well before the heaviest Irish immigration years, the steam-assisted sailing ship *Savannah*

CHILDREN'S ROOM

HICKSVILLE PUBLIC LIBRARY
169 JERUSALEM AVE.
HICKSVILLE, N.Y.

Many immigrants never made it across the Atlantic but were wrecked on rocks off North America or the British Isles. This packet ship Albion *out of Liverpool dashed against the Irish coast in 1822.* (Mariners Museum, Newport News)

had crossed the North Atlantic. By the 1830s and 1840s, a few small, full steamships had done so as well. But it was not until the mid- and late 1850s that steamships came to the North Atlantic in a big way, replacing the sailing packets. Unfortunately, that was a few years too late for the huge Irish immigration of the famine and plague years and just after. But steamships did make it much easier for the tens of millions who came in later years, from Ireland and all over the world.

By the late 1850s, steamships in the 3,000- to 4,000-ton range—three to four times as large as the sailing packets—were making the east-west transatlantic crossing in 10 to 12 days. By the late 1870s, 8,000-ton ships were crossing in seven days. By the turn of the century, 15,000-ton ships were crossing in about six days. In 1906, the 30,000-ton ships *Mauritania* and *Lusitania* were able to make the crossing in five days, and later much larger ships were built. A crossing that, in the mid-1800s, might have taken two months or more, in a pitching, rolling "fever ship" (a ship full of very sick people), might take only a week in the early 1900s. Crowded steerage conditions still often existed in the large steamships, but they were nowhere nearly as difficult as they had been in the days of sailing ships. Passage prices continued to drop, as well. The well-over-two million Irish immigrants who came to America after the famine and plague years had a much easier journey than those who had gone before them.

Arrival in America

During the 1600s and 1700s, the main Irish immigration was that of Protestant farmers, most of them from Ulster. These were people who arrived in America through all the main Atlantic coast ports, and soon headed inland to become farmers again. Some, but relatively few, stayed in the port cities to take up careers as merchants and professionals. Most of those who arrived as indentured servants—Protestants and Catholics alike—also moved inland. Many Irish immigrants moved into the middle Atlantic states—especially New York, Pennsylvania, and Maryland—where they were to form part of the backbone of the Revolutionary armies in 1775. Others moved south through Virginia into the Carolinas, fought the American Revolution on the frontier, and moved out through Cumberland Gap, following Daniel Boone west after the war was won. (More of this in the next chapter.) These early immigrants mainly moved through the many Atlantic ports out into the countryside and to the frontier fairly swiftly and easily. In this, they were helped by the immigrant chains that swiftly developed, as whole communities worked through the process common to so many immigrant groups.

This ease of passage into America changed greatly, and much for the worse, starting in the 1820s. For then the main wave of the huge Irish Catholic immigration began. It was to be ten times the size of that earlier Irish immigration, and in a much shorter time. It was also composed of much poorer people, many of them arriving sick and nearly penniless during and just after the famine and plague years.

This huge new Irish immigration came mostly through the port of New York, rather than through all the main Atlantic coast ports as it had in earlier days. Between 1820 and 1860, American records show that about 5,400,000 immigrants arrived in the United States. Of these, some 3,700,000 or about two-thirds, arrived through New York, with about 550,000 more arriving through New Orleans, at the mouth of the Mississippi River. The rest came through the other Atlantic, Gulf Coast, and Pacific ports, and across the Mexican and Canadian borders. New

York, by then, had become the main American port of entry, and was to remain so right up into the 1920s, when new immigration laws shut off most of the immigration into the United States.

New York had become the gateway to the United States—largely as a matter of geography. Between the East Coast and the heartland of North America lie the Appalachian Mountains. In the United States, there is only one good water route through those mountains to mid-America: that is from New York City north up the Hudson Valley and then west out through the Mohawk Valley, across New York State. The only other way is to go south and into Kentucky through Cumberland Gap, or to go even farther south and go around the mountains in mid-Georgia. Because the new country's main cities and industries were in the north and Middle Atlantic states, the main way west was the northern route.

So the Hudson-Mohawk valley route saw the development of heavily traveled roads, the building of the Erie Canal, and then the coming of the railroads, all during the first half of the 1800s. Irish-American workers were employed in great numbers to build the developing road system. They were also largely responsible for the building of the Erie Canal, finished in 1825. Irish-American workers were also the main labor force that built the whole Eastern and Midwestern portions of the huge American railroad system.

In those days, of the millions of Irish immigrants who came to New York, many stayed. Many others, however, went on into the interior of America. With them came millions of other immigrants—such as the Germans, English, Scotch, and Scandinavians. And with so many immigrants coming into the port of New York, immigrant cheating became a big business there, just as it was in Liverpool in those years.

For Irish and other immigrants of the time their condition on arrival caused a great deal of the trouble. After perhaps two months at sea, the immigrant ships would arrive in New York harbor with a great many seasick, exhausted, half-starved, and often seriously ill people in them. The ships would be boarded by American doctors in the harbor, and the seriously ill people would be taken off and put into hospitals. Then, night or day, the rest of the immigrants would be put into open boats and taken to shore. There they were simply, and with very little inspection, admitted into the United States. They were usually in far worse condition than before boarding ship in Liverpool.

This often made them very easy prey. "Runners" boarded the ships in the harbor and offered to guide their countrymen and countrywomen to safe, secure, clean, honest boardinghouses. Instead, they guided them to boardinghouses run by people who overcharged them, cheated them on exchanging their money for American money, sold them false tickets to Albany and other places farther into America, stole from them, and did whatever else they could to take all they had. It was Liverpool all over again, and worse. In New Orleans and the other main American ports, similar conditions were reported.

New York did little to try to correct this sad state of affairs until the late 1840s. But by then there was pressure from such organizations as the Irish Emigrant Society and the German Society, from many ethnic newspapers, and from some American reform groups. By the late 1840s, there was also fear of plague coming into the American cities from the Irish immigrant ships. In those years, New York turned away several "fever ships," as the plague-carrying ships were called. They had to go north to Canada, there to join the scores of fever ships in the St. Lawrence.

Also, starting in the late 1840s, American attitudes began to change. In 1847, New York State formed an Immigration Commission, which took over the existing immigrants' hospital on Staten Island and opened a new hospital on Ward's Island. They also began searching for a site for a state

From 1855 until the 1890s, most immigrants landing in New York Harbor were sent with their luggage to Castle Garden for inspection before they were allowed to enter the United States.
(Harper's Weekly)

immigration station. In 1855, the commission opened Castle Garden, at the Battery, on the tip of Manhattan Island.

Castle Garden was the main entry point for immigrants from Ireland and all over the world from 1855 to 1892, when Ellis Island was opened. Almost two million Irish immigrants passed through Castle Garden in that period.

Arrival in New York was much easier for immigrants once Castle Garden was in operation. There were still runners waiting to cheat the unwary after they left Castle Garden. There were also abuses in some periods inside Castle Garden, as many people operating food and money-changing concessions cheated arriving immigrants until they were caught. But on the whole, Castle Garden was a great improvement. There, the new arrivals could change their money, make arrangements for travel farther into America, and steady themselves while preparing for their next moves.

From 1892 on, that function was taken over by Ellis Island, the great entry station of the later immigration years, lying out in New York Harbor beyond the Statue of Liberty. In fact, the first immigrant to pass through Ellis Island was a young Irish girl named Annie Moore. But

From 1867 on, Irish immigrants just off the boat could often find work through the Labor Exchange at Castle Garden, as laborers or servants, for example. (By Stanley Fox, *Harper's Weekly*, August 15, 1868)

those years were past the main wave of Irish immigration, and the story of Ellis Island is better told in other books.

Here, then, are the Irish-Americans, arriving in two main waves and a continuing long, steady flow, over a period of 300 years. There are the early immigrants, spreading out to the frontier as it moved all the way across the continent to the Pacific Ocean. There are those who came off the timber boats to Canada, and then south to the United States, by land and coastal ship. There are the millions who later came directly by ship, some staying in the coastal cities; some moving west, as they built the roads, canals, and railroads; some coming up the Mississippi River from New Orleans; some going West seeking gold. In the next chapter we look at their life in the new country.

5

The Early Irish-Americans

For many early immigrants from Ireland, America meant the rough, hard life of the new American frontier. By the mid-1700s, there were Scotch-Irish settlements on the whole length of that frontier, from Maine to Georgia.

In New England, the settlers moved out into western Massachusetts and north into Maine, facing the Iroquois to the west and the French and their Native American allies to the north and northwest. The Iroquois and other Native American lands were to be an effective western boundary until after the American Revolution. British policy was to make alliances with the Iroquois and others against the French, their great enemies in North America and the world. Scotch-Irish settlers were with the British who went north against Quebec itself, during the long British-French struggle for North America that ended only with the French and Indian Wars in 1763.

But the main Scotch-Irish settlement was not to come through New England, although many of Ulster's Presbyterians had expected that to be the most natural entry into America. New England was welcoming at first, and some Scotch-Irish ministers and congregations seeking religious freedom felt it logical to join others who had fled to America to practice their dissenting Protestant religions in peace, as had the Puritans who came to New England first. However, the reality was different. As it turned out, the arriving Scotch-Irish and their ministers had little in common with those who had settled New England earlier—except for a strong tendency to dislike and persecute any religion other than their own. The Puritans criticized and discriminated against the new Scotch-Irish arrivals, the Presbyterian Scotch-Irish sharply critized Puritan religious practices, and New England was soon not a welcoming place.

It was also a question of where the ships went. The main transatlantic trade was from ports south of New England. Settlers from Ireland found far more packet ships sailing to such ports as Philadelphia and Baltimore than to Boston, and more favorable fares as well.

The attitudes Irish immigrants encountered were important in another way as well. Where provincial governments, such as those of Pennsylvania and the Carolinas, wanted to attract Irish settlers to people the expanding frontier, they were eager to provide land on favorable terms. Also, local land speculators everywhere were very willing to sell land acquired for next-to-nothing to new settlers. That was especially so where provincial governments encouraged such land sales.

On the Pennsylvania Frontier

In the 1720s, Pennsylvania became a magnet for tens of thousands of Scotch-Irish settlers, for several reasons. The main American transatlantic trade with Ulster was through Philadelphia, the frontier was expanding west and south, and the tradition of religious liberty in Pennsylvania was strong. Quaker William Penn had founded Pennsylvania as a center of religious and political freedom in the 1680s. In the 1720s, Pennsylvania was continuing that tradition, and the Scotch-Irish were very welcome in-

Many Irish Protestants—especially dissenters from the English form of Protestantism—came to Pennsylvania at the urging of James Logan, William Penn's Irish secretary.
(Library of Congress)

deed. So were the Germans, Welsh, English, and others who flocked into the colony.

Most of the Scotch-Irish immigrants sought land, and moved to the expanding frontier to find it. Some of the earliest settled near Philadelphia, but large numbers soon went beyond, into the Cumberland Valley. During the next half century, until the American Revolution, they moved farther west, through the Allegheny Mountains, into central and then western Pennsylvania. In the process, they and the other people on this part of the American frontier created the Pennsylvania Road, running from Philadelphia out through Harrisburg and over the mountains to Pittsburgh.

The Scotch-Irish were to stay in western Pennsylvania, and throughout the rest of Pennsylvania as well. From the Scotch-Irish frontier settlements would come many of the soldiers of the Pennsylvania Line regiments that formed the backbone of Washington's Continental army. Later, their children's children would help make western Pennsylvania part of America's coal and steel heartland.

Moving with the Frontier

Large numbers of Scotch-Irish immigrants took another, at least as important, way through Philadelphia and out to the American frontier. Over the course of that same half century, from the 1720s through 1775 and the American Revolution, tens of thousands of Scotch-Irish immigrants and Americans of Scotch-Irish parentage followed the frontier south and west along the broad valleys on the eastern side of the Appalachian Mountains. These frontier people began to create what was later called the Great Pennsylvania Wagon Road. Their path—and their path of settlement—moved west out of Philadelphia through Gettysburg, and then south through Virginia and what is now eastern Tennessee. In 1775, they began to move west through Cumberland Gap, on the Wilderness Road that Daniel Boone and his axemen cut for them in that year. After the Revolution, as the new nation burst out beyond the Appalachians, hundreds of thousands of pioneers poured through Cumberland Gap, while millions more were to pour through Pittsburgh on the way west.

Those who kept moving south with the frontier found their way into the Carolinas and Georgia. Their portion of the westward movement led around the mountains to the south, and then out through Alabama,

Mississippi, and west to Texas and the Southwestern states. And so it happened that much of the expanding American frontier in the South and Southwest was peopled by the descendants of the early Scotch-Irish immigrants.

A smaller, but substantial Scotch-Irish emigration directly to the Carolinas and Georgia also occurred. This was not so much a matter of transatlantic trade, but rather of provincial governments and local land speculators welcoming the new settlers to strengthen their frontier positions against the Native Americans in the region.

The Scotch-Irish settlements did provide additional strength on the frontier. They also provided a continual, running war with the Native American tribes whose lands they were taking—or that speculators were taking and selling to the new settlers. That long war led to friction between the Scotch-Irish and other (mostly German) settlers in the early days in Pennsylvania, for William Penn's approach was to make peace with the Native Americans and respect their land rights. It also led to friction between the new settlers and the British government, for British policy was to make alliances with the local peoples against the French and their local allies. That long-term policy of alliance was one of the key reasons the Mohawks fought on the British side during the Revolution, and why so many of the Scotch-Irish and other settlers on the frontier fought against the British.

There was also friction directly between the Scotch-Irish on the frontier and the colonial governments. There were armed confrontations in Pennsylvania in the 1760s, and a small civil war in the backcountry of North Carolina between 1766 and 1771. There, the "Regulators," a local militia composed mainly of Scotch-Irish settlers, were in revolt against the colonial administration. At the Battle of Alamance, the Regulators were defeated, and their movement ended. Afterward, many of their leaders were hanged. But Alamance did not end the struggle. Within four years, it would break out once again, in the American Revolution.

The American Revolution

There were Irish-Americans on both sides of the American Revolution. The most highly visible of them to us today are those who fought on the revolutionary side. But this is mostly because they were the winners, and have become honored founders of the American nation. We know that largely Irish regiments formed the Pennsylvania Line, part of the heart of Washington's Continental army. But we also knew that the British were able to form the Volunteers of Ireland Regiment in Philadelphia. In New England, the cradle of the Revolution, almost all frontier Irish-Americans supported the Revolution. But in 1775, the British were able to form the Loyal Irish Volunteers in Boston.

Most of those Irish-Americans who fought and supported either side were the people of the Ulster Protestant migration of the 1700s. And most of these were frontier settlers, who supported the Revolution, though in the Carolinas there were many Irish-American Loyalists even on the frontier.

However, the Irish-American migration had included many kinds of people from all over Ireland, carrying many kinds of beliefs. For example, tens of thousands of poor Catholics had come, many of them later converting to Protestantism. So had a good many well-to-do Protestants and Catholics, some of whom settled in the port cities. Many of these quite naturally supported the British as the legitimate government of the colonies.

In Pennsylvania, though, where so much of the war was fought, the overwhelming majority of Irish-Americans—city and country alike—supported the Revolution and were willing to fight for it. American General Light-Horse Harry Lee called the Pennsylvania Line the "Irish Line," and for good reason. It included such Irish-American soldiers as Colonel Richard Butler, born in Dublin in 1743, who commanded the American forces that stormed Stony Point during the Revolution; Colonel Delany Sharp, born in county Monaghan, of the Fifth Pennsylvania; Irish-born Dr. Edward Hand, a lieutenant colonel during the Revolution and later a major general; and General William Irvine, commander of the Sixth Pennsylvania.

The Irish-American contribution went far beyond Pennsylvania. In May, 1775, before the Declaration of Independence, Scotch-Irish settlers in Mecklenburg County, North Carolina, were among the first people in the colonies to declare themselves free of British rule. Farther north, the Irish-American frontiersmen of New England and New York were a large part of the army and militia that forced British General Burgoyne's surrender at Saratoga. Key roles in the war were played by such soldiers and sailors as Irish-born General Richard Montgomery, killed in the attack on Quebec in 1775; General John Sullivan of Massachusetts; and Captain John Barry, commander of the USS *Lexington*. While there were

General John Sullivan of Massachusetts was one of many Irish-Americans who played an important role in the American fight against the British.
(Library of Congress)

Irish-Americans on both sides during the American Revolution, it is clear that the main Irish-American contribution was to the Revolutionary side. This pattern of involvement in the affairs of the American nation was to continue during the early years of the new United States.

In the New United States

As the new nation burst out beyond the Appalachians on the long westward surge that would take Americans to the Pacific Ocean, Irish-Americans began to experience great political and material success. Many Scotch-Irish were still the poor settlers of an ever-changing frontier, but now they were people able to generate political power.

By 1800, large numbers of Scotch-Irish were heavily involved in the political life of the country. In that year, most Irish-Americans supported Thomas Jefferson for the presidency, helping to elect a man who would decisively move the country west with his Louisiana Purchase. By 1829, the seventh American president was Andrew Jackson, son of Scotch-Irish

The first Irish-American president was Andrew Jackson, who won with heavy support from Scotch-Irish voters on the new American frontier.
(Lithograph by Lafossé after daguerreotype by M. B. Brady, Knoedler, 1856, Library of Congress)

immigrants from Carrickfergus, in northern Ireland, and the first president with Scotch-Irish roots. Jackson was a person of the American West, a backwoodsman and an Indian War fighter whose strongest support came from the Scotch-Irish settlers of the new frontier. This was the frontier that Daniel Boone's axemen had opened, out beyond the mountains to the Mississippi, and from the Great Lakes to New Orleans.

There was a dark side to Scotch-Irish success, too, a side fed by bigotry and hatred. On the frontier, the dark side expressed itself as a continuing war against the Native American peoples, who, in trying to keep their land, resisted the new nation's push west. The most widely known example of this was the state of Georgia's expulsion of the Cherokees from their land and the forced march of thousands of Cherokees to Oklahoma. That march is known as the "Trail of Tears," for many of those unjustly forced to move died on the way. In fact, the United States Supreme Court had upheld the Cherokees' right to their own land, but President Jackson refused to enforce the ruling of the Supreme Court, allowing Georgia to expel the Cherokees. The attitudes and practices of those who expelled the Cherokees and others were to provoke war after Indian war for most of the 1800s.

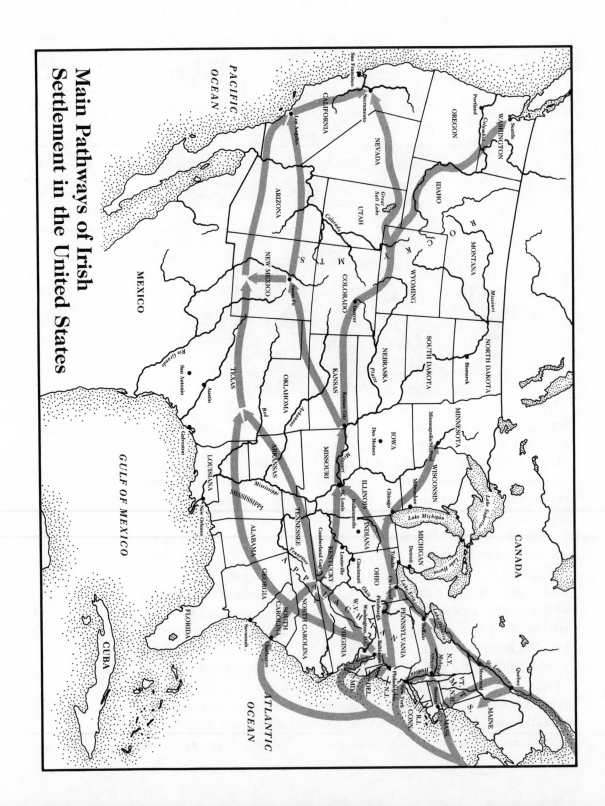

Main Pathways of Irish
Settlement in the United States

There was a dark side in the cities as well. For even as Scotch-Irish-Americans began to merge into the general American population of the time, large-scale Catholic emigration from Ireland began. With that emigration, a great deal of bitterness, fear, and hatred surfaced among American Scotch-Irish. Thousands joined the anti-Catholic movements of the time. Soon they became the backbone of the American Protestant Association. Starting in the 1830s, Irish Protestant marchers in American cities celebrated the Battle of the Boyne, when William of Orange defeated the Catholic armies. Such marches often provoked anti-Catholic riots. In the 1840s, there were anti-Catholic riots led by Protestant "Orangemen" in city after city. The worst was the burning of the Ursuline Convent in Charleston, outside Boston, in 1834, and the church-burning Philadelphia riots of 1844. As late as the 1870s, Irish factional riots continued to erupt in several cities, including New York.

As has so often happened in the United States, political events in the Old Country greatly affected American events. The main trend to come was an extension of the long Catholic-Protestant battle to the United States. Yet there was also a small but strong attempt by many Irish-Americans to build ties between Irish Catholic and Irish Protestant Americans against a common British enemy in the Old Country. Boston's Irish Society was, from the early 1740s, a united Protestant-Catholic organization. So were the many chapters of the Friendly Sons of St. Patrick, and such organizations as Philadelphia's Hibernian Society For the Relief of Emigrants from Ireland, organized in 1790. In the United States, as in Ireland, it has never been as simple as Catholic against Protestant, a war to the death.

Into the Mainstream

Scotch-Irish-Americans in the early years of the United States had little to do with the Old Country. With independence won, and the new nation moving west, it was life in America that mattered most. As with so many of other new Americans they were merging into the American mainstream and losing a good deal of their Old World identity. In western Pennsylvania, western New York, and out along all the rivers that fed the great Mississippi, a very new world was coming into being. Most people were no longer thinking of themselves first as Scotch-Irish, English, Scottish, or Welsh, but rather as Americans with those backgrounds.

Scotch-Irish-American
Cyrus McCormick's
reaper revolutionized
farming by allowing
farmers to harvest their
crops by machine.
(Library of Congress)

Later, the Germans, Scandinavians, and Irish Catholics would follow much the same process, and later yet, all the other peoples of the world, coming to live as Americans.

That process of "Americanization" was clear in the matter of religion. The main body of the Scotch-Irish emigration of the 1700s had been Ulster Presbyterian, a strong, community-centered kind of Protestant belief and church organization. Indeed, much of the early Scotch-Irish emigration was led by Presbyterian clergymen. There were ministers in the early Chesapeake Bay settlements. And as early as 1714, Presbyterian ministers William Homes and Thomas Craighead had emigrated to Boston, beginning a substantial immigration chain. There were missionary colleges, starting with the Log College, at Neshaminy, Pennsylvania, and including the College of New Jersey, founded in Elizabeth, New Jersey, which later developed into Princeton University.

Yet in America even this very strong church and set of beliefs found the going hard. As America changed and moved, so did people's beliefs and church affiliations. Presbyterians often became Methodists or Baptists—or dropped church affiliation entirely. Presbyterianism itself changed too. The churches often became less centers of community life and more narrowly focused on matters of religious belief and practice.

The process of merging with the American mainstream is, in all ethnic groups, much helped by success in the new country. A people who could claim three early American Presidents—Andrew Jackson, James K. Polk, and James Buchanan—were achieving that kind of American success. Later, there would also be William McKinley and Woodrow Wilson, as well as a host of other notable Americans. There were five Irish-American signers of the Declaration of Independence, with ancestors from all over Ireland. There were the Confederate General Stonewall Jackson, the Ulster-born Pittsburgh financier Thomas Mellon, the inventor Cyrus McCormick, and many, many more of early Irish-American descent.

There was some maintenance of early Irish-American identity, in later organizations and celebrations. But the great mass of early Irish-Americans were, by the late 1800s, beginning to merge into the American mainstream. The process was well on its way when the great second wave of Irish immigration began to arrive—the millions of Catholic Irish, who in their own time and in their own way became Irish-Americans.

6

The Main Wave of Catholic Irish-Americans

All we want is to get out of Ireland . . .
We must be better anywhere than here.
An anonymous Irish emigrant

In the second quarter of the 1800s, the main wave of Irish Catholic immigration began. It was to swell into a flood during the famine and plague years of the late 1840s and early 1850s. Afterward, immigration tapered off somewhat, but remained heavy for the rest of the century. Scotch-Irish immigrants continued to come to America, as well, all during this period, and in the tens of thousands. But their numbers were small compared to the millions of Catholics—mostly Celtic-Irish, who were than pouring into the United States.

In Ireland, the great majority of these new immigrants had made their living on the land. Their holdings were very small, and often life itself depended on the potato crop. But sometimes they raised farm animals, and several other kinds of crops as well. Although these were small, poor, and often rather unskilled farmers, they certainly were farmers.

Yet in the United States, only a very small proportion—at most 10 percent—of these new Irish immigrants became farmers. That 10 percent figure is, of course, very easy to misunderstand, for 10 percent of nearly 2 million immigrants during the period of heaviest immigration is still about 200,000 new Irish-American farmers. But in America as it was then, with enormous amounts of land ripe for the taking, far more new Irish-Americans might have been expected to take up farming. The millions of Germans who came in those years moved very heavily into farming, as did the hundreds of thousands of Scandinavians who came a little later.

Some historians have thought that, after the bitter famine and plague years in Ireland, the new Irish immigrants had no more taste for farming. Others have felt that most of them arrived far too poor to go on into America, and to buy land, tools, and seed. There is good reason to think that it was also a matter of how the new immigrant chains formed. Many poor new Irish immigrants found unskilled work in the cities, developed related skills and trades, and then brought others to join them. This is a pattern common to most other immigrant groups as well. Some have even guessed that these new Irish immigrants were somehow inclined to develop tight, church-centered communities—and that the vastness of their new country drove them together into the cities. This last, of course, never stopped any of the other farming peoples who came to America from becoming farmers again, when land was available.

None of these above reasons completely explain the huge Irish settlement into America's cities rather than on the American land. But that is, indeed, what happened. From the 1830s and 1840s on, most of the new Irish immigrants settled in the cities. From there, they began to follow a wide variety of city- and commerce-related occupations, and to help build the new continent wide, industrial America that was being born.

In the Cities

The Irish immigrants coming into American cities in those years were mainly poor and unskilled people. In this, they were like many of the immigrants from southern and eastern Europe who were to come to America, starting in the late 1800s and through the early 1920s. Like those later immigrants, these new Irish-Americans were forced to take the worst jobs for the least pay, and to live in the worst neighborhoods, often in terrible conditions. In New York City, most lived on the Lower East Side, in the areas along the southern part of Manhattan facing the East River. Here, such neighborhoods as Five Points soon became notorious for their living conditions, crime rates, and death rates. Here is Charles Dickens, writing in *American Notes*, about his visit to the Five Points neigborhood:

> This is the place: these narrow ways, diverging to the right and left, and reeking everywhere with dirt and filth. Such lives as are led here, bear the same fruits here as elsewhere. The coarse and bloated faces at the doors, have counterparts at home, and all the wide world.

*Some poor Irish im-
migrants in New York
earned a living—of
perhaps $6 or $7 a
week—as ragpickers,
using dogs to help them
pull their carts to where
they could sell rags
plucked out of the city's
garbage.*
(By Arthur Boyd
Houghton, *Harper's
Weekly*, May 7, 1870)

. . . What place is this, to which the squalid street conducts us? A
kind of square of leprous houses, some of which are attainable only
by crazy wooden stairs without. What lies beyond this tottering
flight of steps, that creak beneath our tread?—a miserable room,
lighted by one candle, and destitute of all comfort, save that which
may be hidden in a wretched bed. Beside it, sits a man: his elbows on
his knees: his forehead hidden in his hands. "What ails that man?"
asks the foremost officer. "Fever," he sullenly replies, without look-
ing up. Conceive the fancies of a fevered brain, in such a place as
this!

People in places like Five Points lived in anything with a
roof—rundown factory buildings, broken-down old frame houses, and in
what were later known as "old law" tenements. These were tremendously
overcrowded apartment buildings, with no central heating, no hot water,
poor toilet facilities out behind the houses, and hardly any air. Most of the
rooms were inner rooms, without windows to the outside. There was only a
small airshaft a few feet across to supply air to the inner parts of the
buildings. Later in the century, new laws forced builders to supply air
space for the inner rooms, but for more than half a century Irish-
Americans and other poor immigrants lived miserably in these tenements.

In New York, as in other American cities throughout the country, the
new Irish immigrants worked in many occupations, most of them low-

paying. Very soon, large numbers of Irish-Americans moved into all of the building trades, where many of their descendants have stayed until today. Hundreds of thousands of Irish-Americans were literally some of the people who built New York—the laborers, helpers, haulers, masons, bricklayers, plasterers, carpenters and tunnelers who built the houses, office buildings, factories, streets, sewer lines, streetcar lines, and then train lines that were the city. They worked for others—for private companies and the city itself. Later, some worked for themselves, as well, as contractors and builders. They grew their businesses side by side with the power of the Irish-American politicians and labor leaders who worked with them.

Many Irish-Americans worked in transportation, as drivers, stable hands, and freight haulers. They also did related work, as longshoremen, shipyard workers, mechanics, and warehouse workers. Many toiled in the restaurant industry, as waiters and bartenders, and others worked in the garment industry. Still others began to move into a wide range of government jobs, such as police officers, firefighters, and inspectors and clerks of all kinds. Irish-American women, unskilled and discriminated against be-

In the summer, Irish-Americans living in New York City's airless "old law" tenements found some relief on the docks, with fresh air coming in off the water. (By Thomas Hogan, *Harper's Weekly*, August 22, 1868)

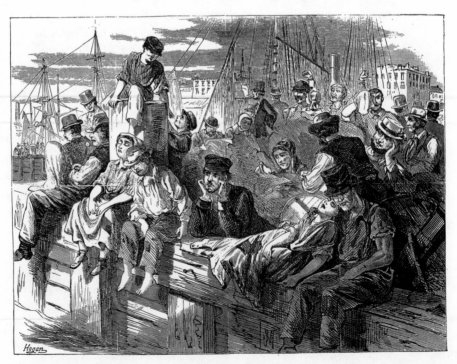

cause they were women, often worked at even lower-paying jobs, as domestic servants, waitresses, and laundry workers.

New York City was the main port of entry for Irish immigrants. It soon became the largest "Irish" city in the world. But many other American cities soon acquired large Irish-American populations too. In Boston, Irish workers early formed communities in such areas as the North End. With the coming of the huge new wave of plague and famine immigrants, South Boston became much like New York's Irish Lower East Side. In other parts of New England, Irish-American workers followed the work available into such textile mill towns as Fall River and Lowell, Massachusetts.

Throughout the new country, Irish-Americans moved into the cities, often following early canal, road, and railroad builders who had paved the way by starting small communities. Once immigrants settled in any area and found they could make some sort of living there, they sent money home so that others in their families could come to join them. So it was that an Irish-American who settled in New York as a construction worker or waitress might, in a few years, be joined by scores of other family members, and perhaps a little while after that by hundreds of others from

Large department stores hired many young Irish women to work as clerks or, as here at A. T. Stewart's on New York City's Broadway, as seamstresses in the sewing room.
(By J. N. Hyde, *Frank Leslie's*, April 24, 1875)

the immigrant's home village or county in Ireland. In the same way, a few Irish wanderers moving south over the Canadian border, or west to Buffalo building the Erie Canal, or out to Chicago building the railroads, were founders of large Irish-American communities in cities along the way.

Building the Way West

To a large extent, it was the explosive growth of the new United States that made the huge Irish immigration possible. There were good reasons to leave Ireland; but it was possible to come to America because there were jobs. Jobs building the Erie Canal and other waterways of the East; jobs building the huge road and railroad networks of the new country; jobs in the new industries created as the country grew. The work was hard, as dozens of folk songs testified, such as this one:

> Every morning at seven o'clock,
> There were fifteen tarriers (drillers) working at the rock,
> And the boss comes along, and he says kape [keep] still,

European immigrants, many of them Irish, built the railroads west from the Mississippi, while Chinese laborers build east from the Pacific. Here the two groups build the last mile of the railroad spanning the continent. (By A. H. Waud, Harper's Weekly, May 29, 1869, Library of Congress)

And come down heavy on the cast iron drill,
And drill, ye tarriers, drill!
Drill, ye tarriers, drill!
It's work all day, and no sugar in your tay [tea],
And drill, ye tarriers, drill! And blast! And fire!

As early as 1817, Irish-American workers were helping build the Erie Canal. The canal, joining the Hudson River at Albany to the Great Lakes at Buffalo, opened the whole way west to commerce. From its completion, in 1825, all the produce of the American heartland could be shipped out to New York and the world. With the canal in place, New York soon became by far the main American port, and a world city. This, in turn, created enormous numbers of jobs, in New York, all the way along the route of the canal, and even farther west. This meant the start of Irish-American communities in such cities as Albany, Rochester, Buffalo, and out along the Ohio River to the Mississippi. Soon there were many other canals, as well, and many major roads, such as the National Road from Washington west. All of them employed large numbers of Irish-Americans, and all of them helped spread the new immigrants throughout the country.

The great American railroad system began to be built in the 1830s, and it was Irish-Americans who built a very large part of that system. That it happened that way was entirely logical; they were already canal and road builders by then. Tens of thousands of Irish-Americans worked building the railroad system that had spread all over the country east of the Mississippi by the time of the Civil War. Irish-Americans were also the great majority of the workers who built the eastern half of the Union Pacific, the first transcontinental railroad, which was finished in 1869.

The Westerners

Some Irish-Americans did not work their way West building the roads, canals and railroads. Instead, they moved directly from one side of the continent to the other. Among these were the "forty-niners," the people of the great California gold rush of 1849, and those who followed them West in later years.

Thousands of Irish-Americans were in the first wave of gold seekers. Many came by ship to Panama across the narrow neck of land there, and then up the Pacific coast to California. Some took the long route overland through the American Southwest. Many took the Oregon-California Trail across most of the continent. Some found gold, though none made enormous gold strikes in the early days. What many *did* do was to go into some of the very same occupations as other Irish-Americans farther east. But with different results. In New York, you might become a bartender and perhaps open your own saloon after a while. But if you went out to San Francisco in gold rush days, you might wind up owning the Parker House and the Jenny Lind Theater, as Tom Maguire did.

Later on, some Irish-Americans did make major silver strikes, in Virginia City, Nevada. The Bonanza Mine was the basis of several great Irish-American fortunes, including that of the family of John Mackay.

But far more western Irish-Americans became builders, politicians, law officers, and teamsters than became gold or silver millionaires. Far more became mine workers than became mine owners. On the whole, though, western Irish-Americans did far better economically than those in the rest of the country, at least until the gold and silver began to run out.

Joining the many new Irish immigrants in the West were many Irish-Americans from previous waves of immigration. There were so many Scotch-Irish settlers in the West that their accent, Americanized over the years, formed the basic pattern of speech in the regions beyond the Appalachians, and especially beyond the Mississippi River. The "cowboy culture" of the West owes much to these Irish-Americans. The popular song, "Streets of Laredo," for example, was originally a song about a young soldier from Tipperary, serving "far away" in the county of Cork.

No Irish Need Apply

For the huge wave of new Irish Catholic immigrants, discrimination was to be a fact of life for generations. These were Irish Catholics, coming to a land dominated by the same kinds of English and Scotch-Irish Protestants they had fought with for centuries of cold and hot war in Ireland. In an even wider sense, these were the people of the first very large Catholic immigration into the United States. German, Scandinavian, and other Protestant immigrants could far more easily merge with the earlier American Protestants than could the Irish Catholics. Small wonder then that there was conflict between religious and ethnic groups in the new country. What is surprising is that the ideas of religious freedom and political democracy worked so well, not that prejudice was found in the United States.

In matters of prejudice, everyone is eager to throw the first stone. The new Irish-Americans were discriminated against by many—not all—of the English, Scotch-Irish, and other Protestants they met in the new land. That is a fact. But at the same time, many—not all—western Irish-Americans were bitterly discriminating against the new Chinese-Americans. Ultimately, such Irish-American labor leaders as Dennis Kearney were to lead a huge, murderous anti-Chinese movement in the West. That movement resulted in Chinese exclusion laws, anti-Chinese riots, and the driving of most Chinese-Americans from the farms and industries they had built. Similarly, many Irish-Americans throughout the country saw Blacks as people who might take their jobs, so they did not support freeing the slaves—although many did fight on the Union side during the Civil War.

As early as the late 1820s, the new Irish Catholic immigrants began running into a huge wave of bigotry. That bigotry often went under the name *nativism*, and was accompanied by a wave of anti-Irish, anti-Catholic speeches and actions. One of the most common signs to be seen in those days, and right up through the Civil War, was that described by Patrick Ford, editor of *Irish World*, writing in 1886:

> I traveled footsore day after day through Boston for a place at a dollar
> a week, or at any price. I would see a notice, "Boy Wanted, No Irish
> Need Apply."

In Boston the homes of Irish-Americans were stoned in the late 1820s. In 1834, a mob burned down the Ursuline Convent, in Charlestown, outside Boston. In 1836, *Awful Disclosures*, by Maria Monk, was published. The book claimed to tell of terrible doings behind convent walls, and was a best-seller, as was a second book of "disclosures." None of the "disclosures" in either book were true, but it was the kind of attack that much suited the bigots of that time. In this way it was much like *The Protocols of the Elders of Zion*, a false work used by anti-Jewish bigots later in the century, and even into our times. *Awful Disclosures* was used by nativists against Irish-Americans as late as 1928, when Catholic Al Smith was running for the presidency.

Anti-Irish, anti-Catholic bigotry triggered many riots and burnings, even after the Civil War. There were Catholic church and Irish-American

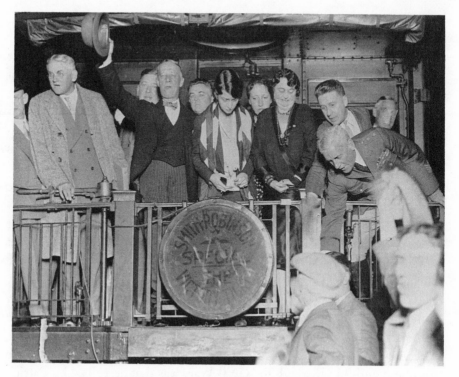

When New York's Irish-American governor, Al Smith (center, waving hat), ran for president in 1928, anti-Catholic sentiment was still strong around the country and contributed to his defeat. (Library of Congress)

home burnings during the Philadelphia riots of 1844, and riots in many cities throughout the 1840s and 1850s. A new party was being born, based on hatred. It was the Know-Nothing party, so called because its members were told to say "I know nothing," when asked about their activities.

The Know-Nothing party became very strong during the 1850s, generating mob action against Irish Catholics and other immigrants as well. Throughout the country, in such cities as Louisville, Cincinnati, Baltimore, and Philadelphia, Know-Nothing mobs attacked immigrants and their communities. Their slogan was "America for Americans." The party became politically strong, too. In the 1854 elections, it won over 75 congressional seats and the governorship in Massachusetts. In many states, the Know-Nothings came very close to winning. In some, such as Maryland and Kentucky, the Know-Nothings were in actual, though not official, control after 1854.

But the Know-Nothings had little to offer a growing America. Where they did take power, they were not able to do anything worthwhile with it. In Massachusetts, for example, their majority lasted only one term, for their administration was scandal ridden and accomplished nothing.

On the other hand, the anti-Irish, anti-Catholic bigotry that produced the Know-Nothings was to persist as a major force in American life all during the rest of the 1800s and far into the 1900s as well. In the 1880s, it generated the powerful American Protective Association, which focused its attack on Catholics around the issue of parochial schools. In the 1920s, anti-Catholicism became one of the main themes of the Ku Klux Klan. The 1928 presidential race of Catholic Al Smith was marred by huge outpourings of anti-Catholic bigotry. Indeed, it was not until John F. Kennedy, very much in our times, that a Catholic was elected to the presidency.

7

Slavery and Civil War

During the middle 1800s, the question of slavery tore the United States apart, and finally brought on four long, bloody years of civil war. When that war came, where people lived had more to do with which side they fought on than anything else. Northerners of many ethnic backgrounds fought for the Union, even though before the war—and even during the war—they might have had different views on slavery. Southerners of many ethnic backgrounds fought together for the Confederacy, even though before the war some of them had hoped to end slavery. Scotch-Irish-Americans in Massachusetts fought for the Union; those in Georgia fought for the Confederacy; those in New York fought for the Union, even though most were fighting to preserve the United States, rather than for the end of slavery.

For Catholic Irish-Americans, most of them recent and poor immigrants, the issue of slavery was never a matter of simple morality and justice, as it was for so many other Americans of the time. Nor did the Catholic church make it a simple moral matter, as did some of the northern Protestant churches. Before and during the Civil War, the Catholic church took no official position on whether slavery was right or wrong. Some individual priests personally opposed slavery, as did Archbishop John Hughes of New York, but the Catholic church did not.

Similarly, individual Irish leaders and a small number of influential Catholic Irish-Americans opposed slavery, but most did not. Daniel O'Connell spoke out against American slavery from Ireland, but on this matter had little influence. Irish-American Senator David Broderick of California opposed slavery, but he was killed in a duel by a pro-slavery politician, effectively silencing that lonely voice.

In an 1856 issue of his newspaper, *The Citizen*, Irish-American writer John Mitchel put one side of the issue this way:

> He would be a bad Irishman who voted for principles . . . which jeopardized the present freedom of a nation of white men, for the vague forlorn hope of elevating blacks to a level for which it is at least problematical whether God and nature ever intended them.

Daniel O'Connell put it quite differently:

> How can you become so depraved? How can your soul have become stained with a blackness blacker than the Negro's skin?

The truth is that the vast majority of Catholic Irish-Americans were against abolishing slavery, and continued to feel that way even during the Civil War—even while almost 150,000 of them were fighting for the Union. One reason for this anti-abolitionist view was fear of competition for jobs from freed Blacks. That fear was present long before the Civil War. Another reason was fear that abolition of slavery would force destruction of the Union, and possible civil war. Yet another reason was the feeling that many abolitionists were also anti-Irish and anti-Catholic, and therefore the Irish Catholics' natural enemies in the United States. And yet another very powerful reason was simply racism, which can take root from many sources, but once started has a strength and acceleration all its own.

Irish-American Soldiers

Although Catholic Irish-Americans fought on both sides during the Civil War, the great majority fought on the Union side. The reason was because most lived in the North; much smaller numbers lived in the Confederate states.

Whatever their feelings about slavery and the other issues of the day, Irish soldiers went off to fight for the Union in large numbers once war came. Over 50,000 came from New York State alone, and almost 50,000 more from the large northern states of Pennsylvania, Illinois, Massachusetts, and Ohio, plus over 40,000 more from the rest of the Union.

In the early years of the war, many enlisted. Some of these were right off the boats from Europe landing in New York. Indeed, some of that large New York State total was really a new-immigrant enlistment. The federal government recruited very actively in Ireland all during the war, as it did in several European countries. There were cash payments, called "bounties," for those enlisting. Recruiting agents promised money, adventure, jobs, land—and a chance to strike at Britain, for Britain was rightly seen as pro-Confederate during much of the war.

Many Irish and other European immigrants were recruited for the Union Army in New York's Battery Park, in sight of the Castle Garden immigration station. (Engraving after M. Jackson, *London Illustrated News*, September 17, 1864, Library of Congress)

A good many all or mostly Irish units fought in the Union army. New York's Irish Brigade was commanded by Brigadier General Thomas F. Meagher. It was made up of three regiments—the famous 69th New York; the 37th New York, known as the "Irish Rifles," and the 88th New York, known as the "Connaught Rangers." (Connaught was one of Ireland's four old provinces, in the west country.) The Irish Brigade fought all the way from early days at Bull Run to the end of the war in Virginia, four long years later.

The list of Irish units in the Union army is very long. It includes the 69th Pennsylvania, which fought at Gettysburg. The soldiers of the 9th Massachusetts, known as the "Irish 9th," were said to have gone into battle flying the green Irish flag beside the flag of their new country. The 24th Pennsylvania; the 116th Pennsylvania; the 90th Illinois, known as the Irish Legion; the 17th Wisconsin; the 10th Ohio—these and scores of other units were all or mostly Irish. The Irish soldiers of the Union army steadily fought through a long, bloody war in their new country, and helped save it from destruction. They also helped to end slavery in America, which is much of what that war was about, although that was not how most of them saw it.

The Third Irish Regiment of the Union Army was named after "our Irish hero" Brigadier General Michael Corcoran, who helped recruit his fellow Irishmen in Boston. (Library of Congress, Broadside Collection, about 1861)

THIRD IRISH REGIMENT

From Massachusetts, and First Irish Regiment for Nine Months' Service.

25 ABLE-BODIED MEN

Wanted to fill up the Company to be commanded by

CAPTAIN WILLIAMS,

Formerly of the MASS. 24TH; now of the 55TH (IRISH) MASS. REG'T.

Come with us and our IRISH HERO,

CORCORAN

Let us carry the American Eagle over the Potomac, down like an avalanche through the land of Dixie, emulating

THE GLORY of the other IRISH REGIMENTS.

$150 Bounty

And all who Enlist will receive the STATE AID.

All Recruits to this Regiment, on signing the Muster Roll, will go at once into comfortable quarters, and receive full rations of the best the market affords.   Apply immediately to

Captain WILLIAMS, or, Lieut. LEONARD!

No. 109 CAMBRIDGE STREET, BOSTON.

Herald Job Office, No. 4 Williams Court, Boston.

Some very well known Catholic Irish-American officers served during the Civil War. Perhaps the best known was cavalry commander General Philip H. Sheridan, child of Irish immigrants, his father a canal and road builder who had settled in Ohio. Another was Colonel and then Brigadier General Michael Corcoran, organizer of New York's Corcoran's Brigade, also known as the Irish Legion, who died in 1863. Another was Colonel Patrick O'Rorke, killed at Gettysburg.

*One of the most senior
and highly respected
Union officers of Irish
background was cavalry
commander General
Philip Sheridan, shown
here with his staff.*
(Library of Congress)

There were some other heroes, as well, who saved lives, rather than taking them. On the battlefields of the Civil War were thousands of dedicated doctors, nurses, and other medical staff people. They are less well known than those who fought, but are at least as much heroes. One such was Mary O'Connell, who as Sister Anthony was one of the best known of the Catholic nuns who did battlefield nursing during the war. She had been educated by the Ursuline nuns in Charlestown, Massachusetts—the same nuns whose convent had been burned to the ground during the anti-Irish, anti-Catholic Boston riots of 1834. Many other Catholic doctors and nurses served as well, such as surgeon Lawrence Reynolds, of the Irish Brigade.

Some Irish Catholics also fought hard for the Confederacy. There were far fewer of them than in the North, but some were organized in all or nearly all Irish units, as in the Union army. At least one Louisiana battalion and several companies were Irish, as were Virginia's company-strength Emmet Guards and Montgomery Guards. Major General Patrick Cleburne of Arkansas was killed late in the war; General Joseph Finnigan fought in Florida.

One of the most famous Irish-Americans fighting for the Confederacy was Scotch-Irish-American General Thomas "Stonewall" Jackson. (By Minnes of Richmond, Virginia, 1863, Library of Congress)

Both sides took enormous losses. Many died; many were seriously wounded. Many were seen as heroes in their day; most just fought and lived or died, as soldiers do. Afterward, a few stayed in the army. Some of these went west to fight the remainder of the Indian wars, from the Canadian border to the Rio Grande. Most went back into civilian life, with or without medals.

The New York Draft Riot

The main Catholic Irish-American role during the Civil War was in the North. It was there that for Catholic Irish-Americans, the worst incident of the war occurred. This was the New York Draft Riot, really a series of riots—in July 1863. Although there were antidraft riots in other cities, the New York riots were by far the worst.

By the middle of 1863, it was no longer easy to find volunteers for the Union army. By then, so many had been killed and wounded that even increased bounties for enlistment did not supply enough men to fight the war. A draft law had been passed on March 3, 1863, providing for forced service in the Union army.

But it was a very unfair draft law. The rich could buy their way out of service by paying a fee of $300, or by providing a substitute. Though $300 was a lot of money in those times, it was a sum many well-to-do people could pay. The poor—including almost all the Irish Catholics—could not raise that $300 to buy their way out of the army, and so were forced to serve.

The new draft law was called unconstitutional by New York State Governor Horatio Seymour, and New York Mayor Fernando Wood. There was also a great deal of anti-Black, antiwar feeling in New York's Catholic Irish community, as in similar communities all over the North. Many had gone to war, but many had stayed behind. Those who had stayed behind were critical of the war, and especially of Lincoln and of every suggestion that the slaves be freed. Many Irish-American newspapers and leaders had opposed the war before it broke out, and some of them gave only lukewarm support to the Union war effort after war broke out. There were many open and influential racists in the community, as well, before and after the draft riots.

During the war many Irish-American newspapers, such as New York's *Metropolitan Record*, were strongly racist and anti-Lincoln. By the middle of 1863 these were part of the "Copperhead" movement, a Northern movement aiming to make peace with the Confederacy and destroy the Union.

An especially inflamed situation arose in New York in the spring and summer of 1863. That April, a bitter longshoreman's strike had been broken. Charges were circulated that free Blacks had been used as strikebreakers. These charges only increased the already rampant racism that existed in New York's Catholic Irish-American community.

In this setting, and with these forces at work, the draft law of 1863 was put into effect. In New York, the first draft list was made public on July 11. It contained the names of 1,200 men to be drafted, most of them Irish and poor. By Monday morning, July 13, mobs had gathered, and soon the rioting began. The New York police were unable to stop the mobs that fought them and took control of the streets.

During the next four days, there was mob rule in New York City. The antidraft, anti-Black rioters stormed an armory, seizing guns and ammunition. They murdered and wounded many Blacks, and burned

In the draft riots of the summer of 1863, mobs attacked everything from private homes to orphan asylums to newspapers, as here New York City's Tribune. (*Leslie's Illustrated Newspaper,* July 25, 1863, Library of Congress)

down the Colored Orphan Asylum. They also attacked and are said to have murdered several Chinese-Americans, for they saw them as "colored," too. There was a great deal of looting, as well.

A full regiment of Union army regulars was sent from General Meade's victorious army at Gettysburg. They were helped by local police, militia, and on the fourth day, by a speech urging peace made by Archbishop John Hughes. Finally, the rioters were stopped.

Later, the draft law was changed. Later, as time passed and as the Union casualty lists lengthened, the huge national reaction against the rioters would soften. Those casualty lists contained the names of so many Catholic Irish-Americans that it was impossible to blame all for what some racists had done in New York in 1863. But the memory of the riots lingered on for a long time—as did some of the racism that helped bring on the riots.

8

Irish-American Politics

As the new American nation grew, so did the political influence of each of the country's large new immigrant groups. Each group in turn developed its own centers of population and political strength, and each in turn began to elect its own kind to office, locally and then nationally. In our time, the process has come to be called *ethnic politics*, as politicians seek the support of as many powerful ethnic groups as possible. But even very early in American history, the process was at work. For example, Scots-Irish frontier ethnic support was important to Scotch-Irish-American Andrew Jackson's election to the presidency.

Ethnic politics was especially important in America's cities, as they grew tremendously and took in great numbers of new immigrants during the 1800s. New Americans, many of them very poor, needed much in the way of help—what today is called a *social service network*. They needed help, for example, in becoming citizens, finding jobs, finding housing, getting medical attention, and working through any forms they had to fill out and other contacts with the law. For all the kinds of help they needed, they soon learned to turn to the big-city political organizations. These operated much like unofficial governments, side by side with the official governments of the cities. In those times, poor people who wanted help received it from their local political bosses. They were as close as the political clubhouse on the next street, and could be counted on, especially if you were of their own ethnic background. Similarly, local businesspeople wanting to get something done also went to the clubhouse, as did people who wanted jobs, especially such politically controlled ones as police, firefighters, and other city services. In return, they had only to support the local political machine.

The large numbers of new Irish immigrants, who had so much to do with the growth of the cities, very soon developed the patterns of ethnic politics. Many Irish-Americans quickly became aware that they could help themselves by taking political power in the cities. What developed out of that awareness was a successful thrust for power, often by thoroughly corrupt Irish-American politicians. They could be counted on to line their pockets, as well as to provide help. But they did provide that needed help, and therefore continued to hold much of the power they seized—until new ethnic groups with new needs and new power rose to challenge them.

In the early 1800s, the Tammany Society was one of New York's two most important political clubs. Until 1820, membership was restricted to native-born Americans, and Irish Catholics were kept out. Indeed, in 1817 there was a riot at Tammany Hall, the club's headquarters, as 200 Irish-Americans forced their way in to protest Tammany's exclusion of the Irish. But from 1820 on, Tammany admitted the new Irish-Americans, and their influence in the club and in New York City affairs began to grow. As large numbers of new Irish immigrants came to America and began to join in local politics, the club became the main Irish-American political organization in New York.

The Bosses

After 1857, Tammany was led by "Boss" William Marcy Tweed, a Scotch-Irish politician who led his mostly Irish Catholic organization to

The New York City political club called Tammany Hall was usually a crowded, noisy place, but never more so than on election night, as here.
(By J. McNevin, *Harper's Weekly,* November 19, 1859)

In the days before voting reform, some polling places were actually placed in saloons, and voters had to work their way past a bar decorated with posters of the "machine's" candidates. (Harper's Weekly, November 13, 1858)

power by electing John Hoffman as mayor of New York City. So began what was later known as the Tweed Ring, which gained control of every part of city government, including the courts. As Boss Tweed himself said: "As long as I count the votes, what are you going to do about it?" The Tweed Ring then proceeded to take as much money as possible out of the city, stealing it in every way they could, from accepting bribes for making crooked city contracts to direct theft from the city's treasury. When the roof fell in, in 1871, Tweed was indicted and convicted. Some of his prosecutors themselves were Irish-Americans.

But in a certain sense the damage had been done. Irish-Americans had been seen as bigots and murderers after the draft riots of 1863, even though almost 150,000 Irish-Americans had fought long and hard for the Union. Now Irish-American politicians were seen as running crooked big-city political organizations even though the clubhouses served real needs, and even though many Irish-Americans helped bring Tweed and others like him to justice.

There was some truth to the charges directed at many politicians, including some who were Irish-Americans. For example, one spectacular

Irish-American John F. Fitzgerald, nicknamed "Honey Boy," was mayor of Boston in 1906. His daughter, Rose, married Boston-born Irish-American Joseph Kennedy, who became a millionaire and later U.S. ambassador to Britain. Their son, John Fitzgerald Kennedy (opposite) became the 35th president of the United States, shown here addressing the Congress in 1962. Behind him is another Irish-American Democrat from Massachusetts, long-time Speaker of the House John McCormack. (Library of Congress)

thief who ran Tammany was Richard Croker, who also ran New York City for most of the years between 1886 and 1901. Croker had been born an Anglo-Irish Protestant, but converted to Catholicism when he went into New York Irish-American politics. He was once tried for murder of a political opponent, was acquitted, but was finally brought down by reformers after scandals were discovered in the city administration. Croker then retired from politics, went back to Ireland, and lived a long, wealthy life there.

There were many Irish-American big-city politicians running "machines" between the end of the Civil War and all the way through the 1930s. One of them was Boston's John F. "Honey Boy" Fitzgerald, grandfather of President John Fitzgerald Kennedy. Another was Boston's James Michael Curley, who was also a governor of Massachusetts. Later, there would be New York Governor Al Smith, the Democratic candidate

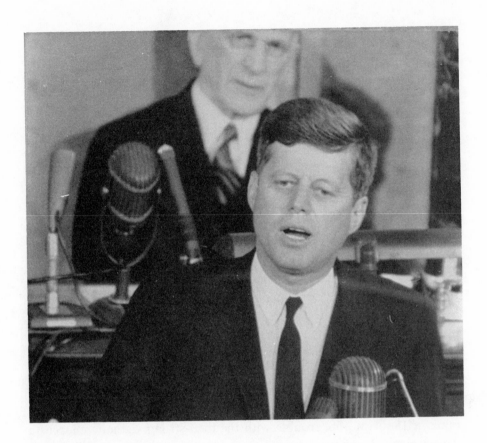

for the presidency in 1928. The truth is that in most big-city political organizations, including those run by Irish-Americans, there was a good deal of corruption. Yet for every Tweed or Croker, there were several Smiths and Kennedys.

With local political power comes wider power, as national politicians seek ethnic group votes. Most Irish-American big-city machines were Democratic party machines, and would remain so until modern times. After the Civil War, as Catholic Irish-Americans began to be elected and appointed to national office, they began to take up national and international issues, as well as local issues.

In the international area, many of the positions taken were greatly influenced by what was happening in Ireland, and in the long Irish-British struggle for that country. For many Irish-Americans the long conflict in Northern Ireland continues to be a major concern.

Irish-Americans and Irish Politics

For many thousands of Irish-Americans, both Protestant and Catholic, the cause of a free Ireland remained vitally important, even as they settled into new lives in America. These were people willing to risk their lives to bring about revolution in Ireland, or for that matter to strike a blow at British rule anywhere. For a much larger number of Irish-Americans, the cause of a free Ireland was important, but scarcely at the center of life. They would give money and moral support, and provide a friendly sea of people in which the revolutionaries could swim, but no more. The numbers of those willing to fight for or support Irish freedom changed over the years, for many reasons. But there has been a powerful Irish freedom movement in the United States, which American politicians have had to recognize and deal with.

As early as 1798, after the defeated Wolfe Tone uprising in Ireland, Irish political refugees began to find their way to America. More came after Robert Emmet's defeated Dublin rising in 1803. Some also came after the defeated "Young Ireland" rising in 1848, which was part of the set of democratic revolutions throughout Europe in that year. Those who came in 1848 ran into trouble with the then-strong Catholic church in America, which was very conservative and attacked them as "red," or radical republicans. Even so, their teachings and example inspired the other Irish-Americans join or support the Irish revolutionary movement.

Circa 1858, the American Fenian movement was formed, which aimed to fight Britain wherever possible, as part of the campaign to free Ireland. During the Civil War, the Fenians prepared for action, organizing groups in the Union forces. After the war, the Fenians organized an invasion of Canada. At the same time, some returned to Ireland, where they unsuccessfully tried to organize a revolution.

The Fenian invasion of Canada failed, as did the attempted revolt in Ireland. Actually, the whole thing was a disaster for the Fenians. About 800 men "invaded" Canada across the Niagara River, near Buffalo, on the night of May 31, 1866. They fought a skirmish with a Canadian force, with small losses on both sides, and then retreated back across the border. Similarly, on June 7, a Fenian force of about 200 men "invaded" Canada across the Vermont border. They retreated, apparently without serious casualties on either side, before any real fighting could begin. The British

In the minds of some Irish-Americans, including this artist, the Fenian "invasion" of Canada was a full-blown battle. ("The Battle of Ridgeway, June 2nd, 1886," Library of Congress)

protested bitterly, American politicians made rousing speeches in favor of freedom for Ireland, and the President ultimately pardoned all American Fenians who had been arrested by U.S. authorities. Some Fenians taken prisoners in Canada were later imprisoned for long terms. The "invasion" of Canada and the failed revolution in Ireland made martyrs and heroes of the Fenians, but did little or nothing for the cause of Irish freedom. On the other hand, it did even more strongly set that cause in the minds of Irish-Americans, who continued to support that cause in the decades to come.

Support for Irish freedom translated into heavy financial support of every Irish freedom movement and leader to this day. Irish-Americans gave money to Daniel O'Connell, sent money for Irish famine relief, gave millions of dollars to Parnell's National Land League, and also formed hundreds of Land League chapters in the United States.

Some Irish-Americans, such as part of the membership of the Clan-na-Gael organization, wanted far more violent action. They advocated bombing, assassination, and other acts of terrorism as a means of helping to free Ireland. Those they supported and joined in Ireland were in that period, much like the people of the Irish Republican Army today, who used terrorist means to try to reach their goals.

A Terrible Beauty Is Born

Throughout Ireland, the fight for Irish freedom continued, led by Charles Stewart Parnell. The British government made some small concessions, especially by helping Irish tenant farmers to buy land. But Britain strongly resisted home rule—that is, the right of the Irish to govern themselves in their own country.

Parnell died in 1891, but even before his death the movement for home rule had weakened. Instead, a powerful independence movement began to form, led by such people as the Sinn Fein Party's Arthur Griffith and socialist James Connolly.

But in mainly Protestant northern Ireland, there was a counter-movement. There was fear that a free Ireland would also be a Catholic Ireland, and that Protestants would be discriminated against. Some Protestants formed the Ulster Volunteers and prepared to fight a new Protestant-Catholic war in Ireland.

There were violent strikes in Dublin in 1913. There James Connolly and James Larkin led in forming the Irish Citizen Army. Meanwhile, Irish revolutionaries formed the Irish Volunteers and themselves prepared to go to war.

When World War I began in 1914, the Irish Volunteers and many other Irish supported the German side. One of their leaders, Roger Casement, went to Germany, seeking support for the Irish revolutionary movement. In Ireland, there was a long tradition of support for anyone who was against Britain. But at the same time, many in Ireland went into the British army and fought the Germans.

In 1916 came the Easter Rising. On Easter Monday, April 24, 1916, Irish Republicans rebelled against British rule, and announced formation of and Irish republic. The rebels took some strategic sites in Dublin, and attacked but failed to take Dublin Castle. Meanwhile, Roger Casement came back to Ireland from Germany, but was immediately captured.

The rising failed. Five days later, the rebels surrendered to the British. Its leader, Patrick Pearse, and 14 other Irish soldiers were hanged by the British, while hundreds of others were deported, many of them to America. Roger Casement was hanged in Britain.

But in another sense the rising did not fail. The poet William Butler Yeats said of these events: "A terrible beauty is born." And something was indeed born—the Irish Republic. For, after the rising, the Sinn Fein became the strongest party in Ireland. In 1918, it led in the formation of the Irish Republic. Eamon De Valera became president of the new Irish government.

The British tried to put down the new Irish government, while in Northern Ireland the Ulster Volunteers made it clear that they would not accept the new republic. Three years of war followed, ending in 1921 with the partition of Ireland. Twenty-six Irish counties became the Irish Free State, still in form partly tied to Britain, but actually an independent country. Six counties in Ulster became Northern Ireland, and remained part of Britain. In 1937, The Irish Free State became Eire (Ireland), and in 1949 it became the Republic of Ireland. But in Northern Ireland, deep problems remain, and there is often much violence. This is due to the sharp disagreement between most Catholics and Protestants over the future of their land.

Continuing Irish-American Support

The cause of Irish freedom has continued to attract tremendous support in the United States, far beyond the Irish-American community. That support continued during the early years of the 1900s, although there were some problems when the United States supported the British-French side in World War I. For many Irish and Irish-Americans, to support Britain in anything at all was to become an enemy of Irish freedom. Many therefore favored the German side in the war, or favored neutrality, until the United States actually entered the war. Then, just as had happened during the Civil War, the great majority of Irish-Americans—though not all—supported and fought in large numbers for the United States. One of the American units was the 69th New York Regiment, in World War I a multi-ethnic regiment, but still largely Irish.

After the war, Irish-Americans continued their very strong support of Irish independence. In 1921, the issue helped defeat the Democratic presidential candidate, James M. Cox, and elect Republican Warren G. Harding. The Democrats were thought to be insufficiently strong in favor of Irish independence, and that was enough to cause a heavy Irish-American swing to the Republican candidate.

St. Patrick's Day parades are often the occasion for showing political support for Irish causes, as here in Washington, D.C., in 1973.
(Copyright *Washington Post*; reprinted with permission of the D.C. Public Library)

After the partial and then complete independence of the Republic of Ireland, Irish politics for a time had little place in the politics of Irish-Americans. But in our time, with the long conflict in Northern Ireland, some of the same questions have returned. Again, some Irish-Americans support violent action, while most Irish-Americans and their leaders prefer a peaceful settlement if at all possible. In our time, Irish and American politics continue to affect each other.

9

Irish-Americans
in the Labor Movement

The list of Irish-American labor leaders includes such people as Philip Murray, president of the Congress of Industrial Organizations (CIO) in the 1930s and 1940s; Terence V. Powderly, Grand Master Workman of the Knights of Labor in the 1880s and 1890s; Peter J. Maguire, early Secretary of the Carpenters Union, who originated the idea of Labor Day; William Z. Foster, organizer of the great steel strike of 1919, and later a Communist leader; Mary Harris Jones—Mother Jones to her mine workers; and thousands of others. Irish-Americans early proved themselves able to build strong unions. In many unions they moved to positions of leadership, even when only a minority of union members were themselves Irish-Americans.

Early Days

It was not always so. Many Catholic immigrants arriving before the Civil War encountered bitter discrimination in employment and even exclusion from some American labor organizations. In Philadelphia, for example, newly arrived Irish weavers in the 1840s were in conflict with established English, Scotch, and Scotch-Irish weavers. Some were refused admission to unions, while others refused to join those unions in the atmosphere of the time. The Philadelphia anti-Catholic, anti-Irish riots of the 1840s were partly due to these labor conflicts.

For the most part, though, the new Irish immigrants readily became part of labor organizations. In the textile mills and footwear factories of New England, for example, the new Irish-Americans joined existing organizations or helped form new ones. So did the Irish-American tailors and construction workers of New York. As would always be true in the world of work, these organizations were not "Irish," but rather multiethnic, for very few employers hired only Irish-Americans. That did

Labor organizer Mary Harris Jones, popularly known as "Mother Jones," is shown here celebrating her 100th birthday in 1930—far from her birthplace in Ireland.
(Library of Congress)

happen sometimes, as when an Irish-American building contractor might hire only the people of his own group. It also sometimes happened in other ethnic groups, as when Jewish-Americans became concentrated in New York's garment industry later on in the century.

Even before the Civil War, Irish-Americans were beginning to become labor leaders. In New York, Boston, and several other cities and areas, there were many Irish-American union members and labor leaders in the garment, longshore, restaurant, construction, mining, footwear, and textile industries.

Sadly, the experience of discrimination rarely keeps people from discriminating against others. So it was for Irish-Americans in the labor movement. They joined other unionists in discriminating against other minority groups, and sometimes actually led the way. An Irish-American, Dennis Kearney, led California's Workingman's party in its murderous attacks upon western Chinese-Americans. Many of New York's draft rioters were Irish-American workers, who accused Blacks of the 1863 longshore strikebreaking. The American trade union movement of the later 1800s and early 1900s, led, in part, by Irish-Americans, bitterly opposed large-scale immigration, even though they were themselves immigrants and the children of immigrants. Union leaders were afraid of immigrant competition, as they were of Black and Chinese competition.

The Molly Maguires

Much has been made of the lawlessness of the Molly Maguires, said to be an Irish-American secret society in the Pennsylvania coalfields in the 1860s and 1870s. The accusation is that during this time the members of the Molly Maguires terrorized the hard-coal-mining fields of eastern and central Pennsylvania, murdering and maiming scores and perhaps hundreds of law officers, mine officials, and anyone else who was in any way against them.

That accusation was developed by Irish-American Franklin Gowen, president of the Reading Railroad, which was a large coal mine operator in the area at the time. Gowen also became a chief special prosecutor of some of those finally accused and hanged as Molly Maguire society members.

Gowen developed his case against the Molly Maguires together with detective Allan Pinkerton, who in turn employed scores of other detectives to penetrate the miner's union and other local organizations. Pinkerton's

Though it is by no means certain that a group called the Molly Maguires actually existed in America, that did not stop 19th-century artists from drawing a meeting of "Molly Maguire's men" discussing a coal mine strike.
(Engraving after drawing by Frenzeny and Tavernier, *Harper's Weekly*, January 31, 1874)

people gave special attention to the local chapters of the Ancient Order of Hibernians, which was the chief fraternal organization of Catholic Irish-Americans all over the country in that period.

The most prominent of Pinkerton's detectives was Irish-born James McParlan, who became a mineworkers' leader, and himself encouraged violence during and after a series of coalfield strikes in the middle 1870s.

There was violence—a great deal of it, and on both sides. Particularly during and after what was locally called the Long Strike of 1875 mineworkers, mining officials, law officers, company police, and a great many innocent bystanders were murdered, beaten, and threatened throughout the coalfields of eastern and central Pennsylvania. That there was much violence is completely clear.

What is not at all clear is who was responsible for which acts of violence, whether the Ancient Order or Hibernians was in any way involved, and whether or not there even was such an American organization as the Molly Maguires. There certainly was an Irish secret society of that name, as there

At the 10th annual convention of the Knights of Labor, a Black delegate introduces the group's leader, General Master Workman Powderly, an Irish-American labor leader.
(Engraving from a sketch by Joseph Becker, *Frank Leslie's Illustrated Newspaper*, October 16, 1886)

were many other Catholic and Protestant Irish secret societies in the 1800s. There was also the testimony of McParlan that such an organization existed, and a list of accused members he produced at eventual trials, and other evidence as well. On the other hand, many legal and labor historians hold the evidence to be very thin and unconvincing. Those who are unconvinced also point out that the accused did not get fair trials. A chief employer served as prosecutor and the courthouses where the trials took place were surrounded by armed company employees. The hysterical anti-Irish, anti-Catholic, anti-labor-union atmosphere that existed at the time in the coalfields made a fair trial highly unlikely—though some of the charges may have been true. The full truth is unlikely ever to be found.

Early in 1876, a series of trials of accused Molly Maguires began. Eventually, 20 men were hanged, and many more were jailed, often for long terms. None of those hanged confessed or named others. Many Americans of the day felt that justice had been served. To many Irish-Americans and union people throughout the country, the men were martyrs, victims who were hanged or imprisoned for being Irish-Americans, union organizers, or both. The bigotry generated on the one side, and the anger generated on the other, caused scars that would take generations to heal.

In the Growing Labor Movement

As America became a huge industrial nation, large national trade unions began to be organized. The first of these was the Knights of Labor, formed in 1869, which included tens of thousands of Irish-Americans. Irish-American Terence V. Powderly became its leader in 1879, and remained so for 16 years, until 1895. The Knights of Labor tried to become a single, big union for all American workers, with all members equal, including women, Blacks, and many professional and business people.

But the idea of a single, equal-for-all, big union was not much liked by many of those in the main trade unions of the day. These were "craft" unions, whose members practiced a single set of skills. Many of those in the craft unions felt that they had a special stake in protecting their jobs by keeping others out, rather than by making common cause with all others who worked for their livings. This was certainly the traditional view of the

Irish-American Elizabeth Gurley Flynn was an active labor organizer in the early 20th century, and had her share of arrests in that anti-labor period, as here in 1917. (Library of Congress)

large numbers of Irish-Americans who had, by then, learned such high-paying skills as metalworking, carpentry, pipe fitting, and all the other skilled trades in such great demand in a fast-growing United States. During the Civil War, relatively unskilled Irish-American longshoremen were ready to riot against Blacks after a defeated strike. By the 1880s, skilled workers were ready to protect their jobs and improve their wages and working conditions by forming the American Federation of Labor. This was the other wing of the American labor movement, and the one that was to win the support of most unionized workers from the 1800s to the 1930s.

Sometimes Irish-American trade unionists are described as "conservative" in both their economic goals and their political views. But the truth is that there have been Irish-American workers and labor leaders in all the major American labor organizations. There have been large numbers of Irish-Americans in the conservative craft unions of the

American Federation of Labor, from its start in 1886 until today. But there have also been large numbers of Irish-Americans in the Knights of Labor, the far-from-conservative Industrial Workers of the World (IWW), and in the Congress of Industrial Organizations (CIO), which split off from the American Federation of Labor in 1938, and merged with them again in 1955. In sum, Irish-American workers and labor leaders have played a great role in the growth of American trade unionism.

10

Irish-American Life

The Ancient Order of Hibernians was the largest of the many organizations the new wave of Irish-Americans developed in the United States. Like the fraternal (brotherhood) organizations of so many other ethnic groups, it served as a meeting place and also an insurance company. And, like so many others, it took up a wide range of other matters important to Irish-Americans over the years. These included the cause of freedom for Ireland, the stimulation of Gaelic Irish culture in America, and a variety of social and educational activities. Many other American groups did the same, including such church-based organizations as the Holy Name Society and the Knights of Columbus. There were also a great many organizations of people from a single locality or county. These, too, were to be found in all the main immigrant communities.

These fraternal organizations served their communities in many important ways. Through the Ancient Order of Hibernians a member might carry life insurance, borrow needed money for personal reasons or to set up a business, find a job, find clients or customers, and keep up strong ties with the culture of Ireland. An Irish-American might send money back to Ireland through an Emigrant Aid Society or an emigrant bank or insurance company. Children might attend classes to learn something of Irish culture and perhaps take classes in the Gaelic language. Singers might join the Irish Choral Society, the literary-minded a literary club, and the sports-minded a sports club. In the widest sense, the fraternal organizations, the political clubs, and some of the trade unions did very similar things for large groups of Irish-Americans, and their activities were often carried out side by side.

The Catholic Church

One of the most important organizations affecting Catholic Irish-Americans was the Catholic church. Certainly some left the Catholic

After Irish-Americans became powerful in big-city politics, many of them moved into government jobs, as police officers, inspectors, or (as here) firefighters. (By Ivan Pranishnikoff, Harper's Weekly, March 4, 1876)

New York Archbishop John Hughes, shown here as a young man, was one of the strong Irish Catholic voices for peace and freedom. (Lithographed by John Penniman, about 1842, Library of Congress)

church once in America, but most who came as Catholics remained Catholics. In religious and community matters, they were greatly influenced by the church.

That was not entirely so in political and union matters, though. Some very influential priests, such as Cardinal McCloskey of New York, were very conservative. They opposed, among other things, the formation of strong trade unions and the growth of such radical political movements as those of the Fenians and the Clan-na-Gael. Not that it went all one way in the Catholic church, either. Some very influential priests, such as Cardinal Gibbons of Baltimore, supported such organizations as the Knights of Labor and spoke for social justice in America.

The Catholic Irish were the first major Catholic group to come to the United States. Because of this, the Catholic church in America was greatly influenced by its early Irish-American membership and leaders. That is why so many Irish Catholic priests, educators, and other leaders have been and often still are so important in American Catholic affairs. The parochial school system, the church leadership or hierarchy, and such schools as the Catholic University of America and Fordham University,

Street evangelist Dwight L. Moody, in the stovepipe hat, worked hard to better the life of Chicago's "street urchins" like these, several of whom are Irish.
(National Archives)

were all organized primarily by Irish-Americans. When large new groups of Catholics began to arrive, such as Italians and Poles, there was much friction, until the Catholic church adjusted itself to its new situation in America.

Some believe that the Irish-American community in America has been socially and politically very conservative, and that the Catholic church is the leading conservative force in that community. But that is too simple an analysis. The Irish-American community is too large, too full of people, forces, and causes for that to be so. There have always been at least two—and often far more than two—views and sets of actions on many issues. Some priests denounced the Fenian cause, while others went north to try to invade Canada. Some Irish-American mine owners fought the emerging unions of the 1800s and 1900s, and in this had the support of their church leaders. Other Irish-Americans helped organize coal miners unions, gold and silver miners unions, the very radical Industrial Workers of the World, and in this had the support of other church leaders. The progressive-conservative arguments within the Irish-American community and within the Catholic church go back a long way and run very deep. They continue today.

The Irish-American Press

Many of the questions before the new Irish-American community were discussed by the very lively Irish-American press. This, too, was very normal. All the major American immigrant groups, and some much smaller immigrant groups as well, developed newspapers and magazines in the early years. These are very important at first, but tend to fade away as the group mixes with and assimilates into the American mainstream. Then—when and if a movement develops to rediscover ethnic "roots"—they grow again, though they never become as important as in the early years.

One of the earliest Irish-American newspapers was New York's *Shamrock*, founded by Edward Gillespy and Thomas O'Connor, which published from 1810 to 1816. Like so many others that were to come later in the century, it spoke strongly for Irish freedom and featured a good deal of news about Ireland. At the same time, it published news of interest to Irish-Americans about their new country. In this way, it was a bridge between the old country and the new, as are most similar publications.

Another early Irish-American newspaper was the Boston *Pilot*, started in 1836 by Patrick Donahue. The *Pilot* focused mostly on news of Ireland, with some American news. It had much success in its early years, reaching a circulation of 7,000 copies. By the 1870s, short of money, it was sold to the Catholic church, and became one of that church's many newspapers in the United States.

The size of the main wave of Irish immigration provided a large set of audiences for the many Irish newspapers started after the plague and famine years of the 1840s and 1850s. There were Irish-American newspapers all over the country. Many focused on Irish news, some trying to balance Irish and American news. Many were independently owned, and these were often strongly focused on the movement for the freedom of Ireland. Some were church-owned, and focused somewhat more on religious matters and religious news, although these, too, often strongly supported Irish political causes.

By the 1860s, there were dozens of Irish-American newspapers, from the many in New York all the way across the continent to San Francisco's *Irish People* and *Irish News*. Most had small circulations, although New York's *The Citizen* claimed a circulation of 20,000 as early as 1854. By 1896, New York's *The Irish World* had a circulation of 125,000, and claimed much more than that in newstand sales, while Boston's *Pilot* had a 76,000 circulation. New York's *Irish Echo* was also a major Irish-American newspaper. The Irish-American press continued to be large and active until the 1920s. Then circulations fell, as Irish-Americans moved fully into American life and somewhat away from Irish and ethnic Irish-American matters.

Into the Mainstream

Gradually Catholic Irish-Americans began to move out into the mainstream of American life, as Scotch-Irish-Americans had before them. It is hard to say when this began. Terence Powderly, for example, was a national labor movement figure in the 1870s and 1880s, although the first great Irish-American playwright, Eugene O'Neill, emerged fully on the national and international stage only after World War I. But there comes a time when a large number of people of any single ethnic background are recognized as leading Americans, rather than as leading Americans of a certain ethnic group. That is so even when the strength of some still comes

Eugene O'Neill, son of acclaimed Irish actor James O'Neill, wrote some of America's finest plays, including Long Day's Journey Into Night. (Copyright *Washington Post*; reprinted by permission of the D.C. Public Library)

In the 1950s, Irish-American Wisconsin Senator Joseph McCarthy led an infamous series of Senate Committee investigations into supposedly "un-American" activities. (Copyright *Washington Post*; reprinted by permission of the D.C. Public Library)

out of their ethnic roots, as when a politician like Al Smith, operating out of an Irish-American-dominated New York City political machine, becomes New York's governor, and then Democratic presidential candidate.

Since the 1920s and 1930s, Catholic Irish-Americans have been fully in the American mainstream. In the world of politics and government, the previous generation had seen James Michael Curley of Boston and the Democratic bosses of a score more of other American cities. By the 1930s, though, Boston financier Joseph Kennedy was Franklin Roosevelt's chairman of the Securities and Exchange Commission, and later ambassador to Great Britain. James Farley of New York was postmaster General. John McCormack of Massachusetts was majority leader of the House of Representatives. So, later, was Thomas P. "Tip" O'Neill, from the same state. Thomas Corcoran was a key Franklin Roosevelt troubleshooter. Frank Murphy of Michigan was attorney general of the United States; later he would become a Supreme Court justice.

There were soon many far more prominent Irish-Americans in politics than these. In our time, they have shown up in every political party and on every side of every major question. The first Irish-American president with Catholic roots was Joseph Kennedy's son, liberal Democrat John F. Kennedy, elected in 1960 and later assassinated. The second was two-term conservative President Ronald Reagan. John Kennedy's brother, Robert F. Kennedy, was attorney general of the United States when he, too, was assassinated. Their brother, Edward M. "Ted" Kennedy, went on to serve for many years as a liberal senator from Massachusetts. Irish-American Father Charles Coughlin was a nationally known bigot in the 1930s, and Irish-American Senator Joseph McCarthy was the leading far-Right conservative of the 1950s. But the two leading Communist leaders of that whole period were Irish-Americans, William Z. Foster and Elizabeth Gurley Glynn. And a potential Democratic presidential candidate in 1968 was liberal Irish-American senator and poet, Eugene McCarthy. The Irish-American heritage keeps right on generating major American leaders.

In American life, the "stage Irishman"—that bigoted view of the Irish-American as a loud, red-faced, drunken, ill-dressed bad joke—has all but disappeared. In the theater, Eugene O'Neill, son of Irish actor James O'Neill, is the greatest of American playwrights. One of his finest works was the three-part work *Mourning Becomes Electra*. Irish-American George M. Cohan, who wrote the popular song "Yankee Doodle Dandy," was one of the most popular stars of the American stage. Laurette Taylor

Former senator from Minnesota and presidential hopeful in 1968, Eugene McCarthy is also a poet, here reading his work in 1971 at the Peace Study House, Church of the Pilgrims, Washington, D.C. (Copyright *Washington Post*; reprinted by permission of the D.C. Public Library)

was a highly respected actress. John McCormack was a world-renowned opera singer—and sang Irish songs to packed houses all over the country as well.

In the movies, Irish-Americans John Wayne, James Cagney, Grace Kelly, Tyrone Power, Bing Crosby, Gene Kelly, and Maureen O'Hara, among others, were great stars. John "Duke" Wayne was one of America's best-known screen stars for 40 years, winning an Academy Award for *True Grit* in 1969. James Cagney was the screen's "tough guy," but he also played George M. Cohan in the movies. Tyrone Power was the great-grandson of one of Ireland's most famous actors, also named Tyrone Power. Irish-American John Ford was one of the finest movie directors who ever lived. He won *six* Acadamy Awards, four for features and two for documentaries. Still on screen, "The Honeymooners," starring Irish-Americans Jackie Gleason and Art Carney, has long been one of America's best-known television shows.

And there are more, far too many to name. Irish-American writer F. Scott Fitzgerald wrote *The Great Gatsby* and many other works. Writer

In a career spanning decades, Irish-American Helen Hayes—shown here in 1978—became the America's First Lady of the theater. (Copyright Washington Post; reprinted by permission of the D.C. Public Library)

James Farrell, who wrote the Studs Lonigan books, and such writers as John O'Hara and James Breslin have long been recognized as some of America's finest artists. In sports, Jack Dempsey, John L. Sullivan, and James Corbett were great heavyweight champions. Joe Cronin, Connie Mack, and Mickey Cochrane are among the Irish-Americans in baseball's Hall of Fame. In more practical areas, William L. Murphy invented the Murphy Bed, and John R. Gregg invented Gregg Shorthand. James J. Farley headed the Coca Cola company, William J. Burns founded his own international detective agency, and William R. Grace founded a huge shipping line. The list of famous Irish-Americans seems almost endless, for by now tens of millions of Americans share the Irish-American heritage.

Irish-Americans in Our Time

The Irish keep on coming to America—the Protestant and Catholic Irish from both Northern Ireland and from Eire, the Republic of Ireland.

Colorado-born Irish-American Jack Dempsey was renowned as World Heavyweight Champion, then retired in glory to run a popular restaurant in New York City. (Copyright *Washington Post*; reprinted by permission of the D.C. Public Library)

Indeed, in recent years the emigration from Ireland to America has strengthened once again, as lack of opportunity in the south and a guerrilla war in the north once again push people out of Ireland across the sea to America.

These new arrivals come to an America that has a long, deep, complex set of Irish-American heritages, going back well over 300 years. It is also an America in which the main bulk of both Scotch-Irish and Catholic Irish-Americans have by now merged deep into the American mainstream—though by no means losing some of their traditional hopes, fears, and loyalties. Irish-Americans today continue to be concerned with the main problems of the Irish in Ireland. Many ethnic groups have the same kind of concern for the "Old Country" and its people. That concern often grows when deep divisions spill over into violence, and winds down when the problems of the old country seem less pressing. As this book is being written, some Irish-Americans express their views by giving money and helping to supply arms to those engaged in armed conflict in Ireland. Others take a different view, supporting attempts to find peaceful

In modern America, St. Patrick's Day is an unofficial national holiday, celebrated by Irish and non-Irish alike, as here in Washington, D.C., in 1973.
(Copyright *Washington Post*; reprinted by permission of the D.C. Public Library)

solutions to Ireland's problems. There are great differences of opinion and action here. What all sides share is the immigrant's concern for the old country, even into many generations in America.

In the United States, after World War II, people of many ethnic groups moved out of the central cities into the outlying neighborhoods and suburbs. It was a time for making some money, buying homes, and settling down, after 16 years of depression and war. In the process, hard-held views were softened, party allegiances changed, and new businesses and professions were entered. After 1945, and continuing today, there has been much more moving of Irish-Americans into the American mainstream than ever before. In modern times, old barriers have disappeared. Irish-Americans have freely entered into every aspect of American life. Religious allegiances remained the same, though. Most Irish-American Catholics have stayed Catholics, and many Protestant Irish-Americans continue to be practicing Protestants, though often in different branches of Protestantism than those their forefathers brought with them from Ireland.

In America today, there are still strong feelings for Ireland and "Irishness" among many Irish-Americans. There is a revival of Gaelic studies and other Irish cultural interests as well. Yet although there continue to be large St. Patrick's Day parades, the main trend is toward that mixing and partial merging that is so much of the shared experience of all the main groups of immigrants from Europe to America. Now, to go across the sea to Ireland is to visit the Old Country; home is here, in the land to the west, beyond the setting sun.

Suggestions for Further Reading

Abbott, Edith. *Immigration: Select Documents and Case Records*. New York: Arno, 1969.

Bailyn, Bernard. *The Peopling of British North America*. Vol 1: *An Introduction*. Vol. 2: *Voyagers to the West: A Passage in the Peopling of America on the Eve of Revolution*. New York: Knopf, 1986.

Bernardo, Stephanie. *The Ethnic Almanac*. Garden City, New York: Doubleday (Dolphin), 1981.

Birmingham, Stephen. *Real Lace*. New York: Harper and Row, 1973.

Bottigheimer, Karl S. *Ireland and the Irish*. New York: Columbia University Press, 1982.

Brownstone, David M., Irene M. Franck, and Douglass L. Brownstone. *Island of Hope, Island of Tears*. New York: Rawson, Wade, 1979; New York: Viking-Penguin, 1986.

Coleman, Terry. *Going to America*. New York: Pantheon, 1972.

Crimmins, John Daniel. *Irish-American Historical Miscellany*. New York: Self-published, 1905.

Doyle, David, and Owen Edwards. *America and Ireland, 1776-1976*. Westport, Connecticut: Greenwood Press, 1980.

Duff, John B. *The Irish in the United States*. Belmont, California: Wadsworth, 1971.

Ford, Henry J. *The Scotch-Irish in America*. New York: Peter Smith, 1941. Reprint of Princeton University Press 1915 edition.

Franck, Irene M., and David M. Brownstone. *To the Ends of the Earth*. New York: Facts On File, 1984.

Greeley, Andrew M. *That Most Distressful Nation*. Chicago: Quadrangle, 1972.

————. *The Irish Americans: The Rise to Money and Power*. New York: Harper and Row, 1981.

Griffin, William D. *A Portrait of the Irish in America*. New York: Scribners, 1981.

Hale, Edward Everett. *Letter on Irish Immigration*. Freeport, New York: Books for Libraries, 1972. Reprint of 1852 edition.

Handlin, Oscar. *A Pictorial History of Immigration*. New York: Crown, 1972.

Hansen, Marcus Lee. *The Atlantic Migration: 1607-1860: A History of the Continuing Settlement of the United States*. Cambridge, Massachusetts: Harvard University Press, 1945.

Jones, Maldwyn Allen. *American Immigration*. Chicago: University of Chicago Press, 1960.

―――. *Destination America*. New York: Holt, Rinehart, and Winston, 1976.

Maguire, John Francis. *The Irish Diaspora in America*. Bloomington: Indiana University Press, 1945.

Miller, Kirby A. *Emigrants and Exiles*. New York: Oxford University Press, 1985.

Miller, Sally M. *The Radical Immigrant*. New York: Twayne, 1974. Part of the immigrant Heritage of America series.

Miller, Wayne Charles. *A Comprehensive Bibliography for the Study of American Minorities*, in two vols. New York: New York University Press, 1976.

Neidle, Cecyle S. *America's Immigrant Women*. Boston: Twayne (G.K. Hall), 1975.

Novotny, Ann. *Strangers at the Door: Ellis Island, Castle Garden, and the Great Migration to America*. Riverside, Connecticut: The Chatham Press, 1971.

O'Connor, Richard. *The Irish*. New York: Putnam, 1971.

O'Donovan, Jeremiah. *Irish Immigration in the United States*. New York: Arno, 1969. Reprint of 1864 edition.

Potter, George. *To The Golden Door*. Boston: Little, Brown, 1960.

Shannon, William V. *The American Irish*. New York: Macmillan, 1963.

Taylor, Philip. *The Distant Magnet*. New York: Harper and Row, 1972.

Thernstrom, Stephan, ed. *Harvard Encyclopedia of American Ethnic Groups*. Cambridge, Massachusetts: Harvard University Press (Belknap), 1980.

Wittke, Carl. *The Irish in America*. New York: Russell and Russell, 1956. Reprint of Louisiana University Press, 1956 edition.

―――. *We Who Built America: The Saga of the Immigrant*. New York: Prentice-Hall, 1939. Reprint of Cleveland: The Press of Case Western Reserve University, 1964.

Woodham-Smith, Cecil. *The Great Hunger*. New York: Harper and Row, 1962.

Index

DISCARD